D1243941

Goose River Anthology, 2020

Edited by

Deborah J. Benner

Goose River Press
Waldoboro, Maine

Library of Congress Card Number: 2020946770

ISBN: 978-1-59713-216-9   paperback
ISBN: 978-1-59713-217-6   hard cover

First Printing, 2020

Cover photo by Betsy Fairfield.

Published by
Goose River Press
3400 Friendship Road
Waldoboro, ME 04572
email: gooseriverpress@gmail.com
www.gooseriverpress.com

Authors Included

Ackermann, Helen: Pages 73–74
Annenberg, Marcia: Pages 25 & 117
Belenardo, Sally: Pages 27, 186, 201
Bennett, Thomas Peter: Pages 9, 136, 212
Bedwell, Mary Ann: Pages 28, 142, 212
Branch, Kristina: Pages 75–76
Brown, Peggy Faye: Pages 169–170
Cane, Monica: Pages 45–46
Chiacchio, Roe: Pages 165–167
Clark, A. M.: Pages 145 & 167
Cochran, Carole: Pages 199–200
Comeau, Philancy: Pages 113–116
Conlon, Sandra: Pages 126 & 146
Covey-Smith, Erin: Pages 56, 141, 159
Dailey, Genie: Pages 49, 143, 198
D'Alessandro, F. Anthony: Pages 70–71, 157–158
de Araujo, Alvaro: Pages 107–108
Derbyshire, Jane: Page 109
Di Gesu, Gerry: Pages 90, 109, 135, 186
Fallon, Tom: Pages 93 & 108
Gallant, Austin: Pages 44, 127, 153
George, Gerald: Pages 3, 134–135
Gerard, E. H.: Pages 49 & 76
Giasson, Mary Ann: Page 111
Gold, Janet N.: Pages 130, 172–173
Grubel, Peggy Iannella: Pages 187–195
Hagan, John T.: Pages 58–60
Hanson, Sherry B.: Page 94
Harnedy, the late Jim: Pages 77–78
Harrington, Ilga Winicov: Pages 11–19
Hartford, Kitty: Pages 91–92
Hill, Andrea Suarez: Pages 106 & 144

Authors Included

Authors Included

In Honor of
Our First Responders.

Special thanks to Sue Campagna for her wonderful help in proofing the book.

Judy Driscoll Winchenbaugh
Rockland, ME

My Story

Here I am, a lonely Boston Rocker in the corner of Coastal Antiques, my home for too many years. I'm dusty, now home to cobwebs and spiders. But once I was grand, so grand; built with love by my master carpenter. Each piece of me cut with care by hand, sanded so carefully (ooh, that felt good) to smooth my bumps. He built me slowly, taking the time to make sure I would last for generations, to bring comfort and reassurance to many.

The carpenter's wife rocked with her babe, comforting his tears, my gentle rhythm lulling him to sleep. As he grew and learned to walk and run, we would comfort the bumps and bruises of a toddler. Then I sat in the corner of his room, forgotten except for the stuffed animals he piled in my seat. But when he became a teenager his mother dusted me off and together we waited for him, sometimes past his curfew. The teenager became a man and moved into his own house.

The carpenter and his wife grew old while I stayed in the empty bedroom of the boy. When the carpenter got sick, his wife brought me out, put me beside his bed. I tried to comfort her while she held his hand as we rocked. After he was gone, I wanted to wrap my arms around her when her tears fell on my wood that he had so carefully stained all those years ago. His wife and I spent many a lonely night each lost in memories of our carpenter.

The boy came back to visit all grown up now; a man, with a wife and a baby. Such joy to see his young family and help his wife comfort their baby. It brought back so many memories of when I was young, before my wood started to creak. When the grown boy and his family went home, my carpenter's wife and I were once again alone. Keeping each other company in the too quiet house.

Sometimes our house would fill with laughter when my

Judy Driscoll Winchenbaugh
Rockland, ME

boy and his family came to visit. His kids climbing all over me, squeezing into my seat together, and rocking me so hard I thought I might break, but listening to their giggles made me feel young again.

When they all went back to their house, my carpenter's wife and I went back to our routine. We rocked each evening to the news, her shows. Until one evening the rocking stopped. The boy came back, rocked with me. Both of us remembering his mother's touch. I miss my carpenter's wife.

Later the boy took me back to his house. His sons climbed on me, but I was too old, I started to break. One day the boy put me in his truck, brought me to a shop. I saw tears in his eyes when he left me there. The store owner took me to his workshop and gave me new nails, new stain. I've been siting here ever since, dust settling, cobwebs forming. Will I ever get a new family? Shh listen, I hear a little boy,

"Momma, look, a rocking chair for my stuffed animals. Please?"

Please.

Gerald George
Belfast, ME

Love, Willie

Always signed "love, Willie,"
he wrote each week a letter home.
When the war started, he hadn't wanted to go
but so many friends had volunteered.
The Fatherland needed soldiers.
Now as he rounded up the hated people,
he looked so handsome in his uniform.

"Don't be afraid for me, my dear," he wrote.
"I am out of the battle.
At first I didn't care much for this job,
but it gets easier.
The first was hardest. Some of us backed out.
But I stayed with my duty. Now the worst
is breathing the bitter stench within the pits."

Sometimes his letters came with wonderful presents
—chocolate, jewelry, toys—
like Christmas, so it seemed to the little ones.
Always a loving father, Willie was.
His children would never suffer from these people
whose heads exploded as he shot them down,
then tumbled them onto the others in the ditch.

Sylvia Little-Sweat
Wingate, NC

Scotland and England

Edinburgh kilts
trooping the royal colors—
bagpipes' bellowed air.

Highlands' wooly cows
graze the green, grow long red coats
for Scottish winters.

Excavated walls—
ancient Roman invasion,
Hadrian's gray stones.

Tower of London—
deigned British reliquary
of reign, blame, and pain.

The London Eye scans
panoramic River Thames—
a thousand-year squint.

Her Majesty's Guard—
red coats, bear hats, polished boots—
Monarchy—measured.

Judy O'Dell
Rockport, ME

The Necklace

She couldn't have been more than 20 years old. I noticed her standing alone as my husband and I entered the room. Curly dark hair cascaded down her back. Her face was not yet fully formed, bearing traces of the young girl she lately was, but there was sadness in her brown eyes. Dressed in a sleeveless, light blue, full-length gown, she could have passed for a Disney princess except for the small tattoo of a cross on her right shoulder. Her only jewelry was a simple gold band on the third finger of her left hand.

The event was a reception honoring Marine Corps Gold Star Families. The term "Gold Star Families" dates to World War I when military families displayed a service flag featuring a blue star for every immediate family member serving in the Armed Forces. A gold star flag would replace the blue star flag if the family lost a loved one in the war.

I broke away from the Marines surrounding my husband, who was the guest of honor for the Marine Corps birthday ball to follow, and approached the young woman. Her name was Angela Rosales, she told me. We must have presented a mismatched pair to anyone observing us. I was wearing my go-to, easy to pack, formal black gown, and a delicate charm necklace that hung into the V-neck of my dress.

I had purchased the necklace in a small shop on Royal Street in the French Quarter in New Orleans when we were stationed there in the late 1990s. I don't particularly care about jewelry. I usually wear only gold button earrings, and my wedding and anniversary rings. For me to purchase a piece of jewelry is a rare event. But shopping on Royal Street is an experience like no other. The shops are small, the shopkeeper is usually present, and the merchandise is unusual. I saw the necklace in a window of a shop about a block from our home. Tiny charms: skulls, ballerinas, ballet

Judy O'Dell
Rockport, ME

slippers, man in a quarter moon, and stars were interspersed with green, purple, blue, and yellow cut glass beads all strung on a dull gold chain. The necklace somewhat resembled a rosary except a larger skull attached to an eight-pointed star with a blue stone center replaced a crucifix at the bottom. The shopkeeper told me it was handmade by a local woman. I sensed some New Orleans voodoo, but it was a quiet necklace, the charms so small that they were unidentifiable from a distance. I liked how the colored beads sparkled when caught by the light.

We had a formal Marine Corps event to attend the night after I bought the necklace. It seemed bizarre to wear a necklace featuring a dangling skull with a formal gown, but over the years, as I wore it to military events, it had come to have a special meaning to me. I saw it as my attempt to ward off the madness that seemed to have gripped the world after 9/11, which I was experiencing second hand. Birthday Balls and formal events went on even as Marines and soldiers were dying, and general officers were expected to attend.

Angela's Marine was Jack. They were childhood sweethearts and were married just before he deployed to Iraq. Her eyes lit up as she described his wide smile, silly jokes, and their off-road adventures in his red Jeep. She had had an email from him for her birthday a few days before he was killed. Tears filled her eyes as she related that. They had plans for their future. She was studying to be a dental hygienist, and Jack was going to finish college when his tour was up. "I really like your necklace," she said. I thanked her and told her of its provenance. After a few more minutes of conversation, a man approached us, put his arm around Angela, and introduced himself as Jack's father. "Tell me about Jack," I said. I had learned that this is the best way to begin what can otherwise be an awkward conversation with parents who have lost their Marine.

Like so many Marines who were killed in combat, I learned that Jack was a golden boy: excellent grades, Eagle

Judy O'Dell
Rockport, ME

Scout, captain of the football team, patriotic, loved his family, proud to be a Marine. Angela nodded and told me that Jack wanted to be a teacher. Jack's father hugged her and said, "Yes, that was his dream." He pulled out his wallet to show me Jack's picture. "You know," he said, "Jack didn't have to go. He volunteered to augment another understaffed unit."

Others interrupted our conversation, and I moved off to circulate the room. The young Marines were resplendent in dress blues, multiple new medals shining proudly from their chests. They talked quietly to the families, and from time to time, I heard laugher as someone told a funny story.

As we moved to join the Birthday Ball in another room, I found myself next to Angela. She again told me she liked my necklace. I thanked her again, and my selfish self began to wrestle with my generous self as I thought about giving her my necklace. Only a few seconds passed as many thoughts flooded my consciousness. Does she really like it that much? Hey, it wasn't very expensive. Would this help her deal with the loss of Jack? What is it like to be a 20-year-old widow? I unclasped the necklace and placed it around her neck. She gave me a tremulous smile. "I'm sorry about your Jack," I said. "I wish I had had a chance to meet him." I hugged her then wiped away tears as I joined my husband at the head of the receiving line. "Are you okay?" he whispered between handshakes. "Tell you later," I said.

A year later, back in New Orleans, I returned to the shop where I had purchased the necklace. I described it, and, by a stroke of good fortune, the shopkeeper had one very similar except that Mardi Gras masks replaced the skulls. I wondered if it had been the skull charms that attracted Angela to the necklace. I think of her every time I wear the replacement and hope that whatever bit of New Orleans voodoo that was in the original necklace protects her from further hurt.

Sister Irene Zimmerman
Greenfield, WI

A Real Barn to Play In

Six-year-old Maddy dumped her toy farmyard
onto the rug to show me. She set up a bright red barn
and surrounded it with a blue feeder trough,
a yellow water tank, two chestnut horses, a dozen
pink pigs, and ten black-and-white Holstein cows.
These she herded out to pasture under the dining table.

Watching her, I remembered myself at her age,
poring over the Sears Roebuck Christmas Catalogue,
longing for the toy animals and barn pictured in it.
My mother had promised to write to Santa for me,
but when I showed her what I wanted, she shook
her head. "It's way too expensive," she said.

"But Mama," I begged, "Santa gets everything free."
She gently but firmly informed me that not even Santa
got things for nothing. "Besides," she added, "you have
a real barn to play in, not like your city cousins."

Maddy caught my attention just then as she grabbed
a black-and-white polka dotted dog. "Time for milking,"
she said. "Let's go get the cows." Snatching handfuls
of Holsteins, she plunked them down into the barnyard.

I smiled at the imagination of this delightful city child
as I remembered playing in the hayloft with my sister—
jumping from the crossbeam into sweet smelling hay,
finding eggs laid by a hen gone AWOL from the hen house,
petting a purring cat as she fed her squirming kittens,
crawling out the cupola door and climbing up the barn roof.

Nothing, I decided, compares to having a real barn to
	play in.

Thomas Peter Bennett
Silver Spring, MD

Florida Footprints

On a morning,
    Gulf beach walk...
Waves of grain,
    America's sea oats,
primal amber waves
    revel in azure sky,
cut by an
    osprey's silhouette.

Tidemarks evoke the past.
    Driftwood and fragments
of shells mark
    an earlier high tide.

In the distance,
    tan-skinned elders
watch children play,
    as all leave
transient footprints in the sand.

Brenda E. McDermott
Searsport, ME

Autumn in Maine

The forests ablaze in colorful coats
welcome autumn's warm September days,
October's first chill of the season.

As I walk down a country road, the papery
leaves of beech trees, metallic bronze of
black oak and intense red maple leaves crease
the forest floor and emit an enchanted scent that
autumn lays claim to.

The woodsy smell of earth, the ripeness
of fallen leaves, the hickory scent of trees
depict Mother Nature's beauty and grace in autumn.

I pass vegetable gardens as they are being cleared.
Aware of the honest aroma of cabbage,
freshly dug onions and garlic before I discover
they're lounging in the sun.

As I turn towards home, I realize that each season
has a unique fragrance: in autumn, the aroma is one
of maturing and fermenting leaves and stalks, in a world
smoldering and withering away in the year's invisible fire.

Ilga Winicov Harrington
Falmouth, ME

The Flag

Peter, with a puzzled look watched on as his grandmother pulled one thing after another from a large cedar chest.

"What are you looking for, Gram?"

"The old flag, child" she murmured bent over.

"What flag? Don't you have a small one in the kitchen in the cup with your pens?"

"No, that one is new. I'm looking for one I had when I was a little girl."

"Oh, you mean, in the old country."

"Yes, I wanted to show the flag to my friends. It is the hundredth anniversary of my old country Latvia."

Peter shook his blond head and said with a smile: "But, you are not that old!"

"No," Gram chuckled, "not quite that old. Just old enough to remember a lot."

Peter's grandmother straightened up with a doll in her hands, a soft expression on her face: "Mārīte," she exclaimed.

Peter looked puzzled at the sad looking thing in Gram's hands. *Well, it has the head of a doll. Sure looks beat up with a crack in the forehead. At least the blue eyes looked fine. The cloth-body had several patches and the doll's drab brown flowered dress was covered with a lopsided maroon sweater. It certainly looked nothing like the dolls Peter's cousins had at their home!*

"This is Mārīte," said Gram. "She was my favorite doll. Aunt Hilda brought her for me when I was a baby, all the way from Berlin. She once looked quite elegant and was special because she could close her eyes and had real eyelashes. But time and travel wore her down. I did try to make her new clothes, but there were only scraps at the time..." she finished with a sigh.

"You brought her all the way from your old home?"

Ilga Winicov Harrington
Falmouth, ME

"Yes, Peter, with the flag," Gram set the doll gently on the bed with the other things she had pulled out and continued rummaging in the chest.

"Aha!" she exclaimed triumphantly and pulled out a round stick about two feet long with a broken end and a small Latvian flag wrapped around it.

When she unwrapped it, Peter said: "Gosh, it looks terrible! It's all beat up. The corner is torn and the colors are completely faded!"

"Yes, it has come far in all kinds of weather." She closed the cedar chest and sat on the bed, gently holding the flag on her lap with a faraway look on her face. Peter loved Gram's stories and made himself comfortable next to her as she began.

The flag's travels began in 1944, when I was about the same age you are now. In the dark pre-dawn morning of September 30th I packed my 2nd grade backpack with two books and my favorite doll. Mama was closing her suitcase and urged me to hurry. After closing the backpack, I slid in the side pocket the Latvian flag to hang as a symbol of our heritage and the place we were leaving. That morning my family and I walked out the door of our apartment in Riga, never to return.

"Why" Peter interrupted. "What happened to make you leave?"

Gram shook her head. "It is a long story child."

That night the bombardment by advancing Soviet troops could be heard in the distance. We were leaving because we knew that if we did not escape, we would face deportation to Siberia. After the first Soviet occupation in 1941 we had found our name on the subsequent second deportation list for Siberia, because someone had denounced us for not being communists. To remain would have been suicidal. Later that day we boarded the German ship Steuben for Danzig (now Gadansk). So began an incredible journey for us and the flag.

Ilga Winicov Harrington
Falmouth, ME

We disembarked in Danzig (Northeast Germany), where we were marched to a train by the Nazis, to travel to a camp in Dresden. But when we got there, we could not stay. The previous night bombing had destroyed the camp. The train then slowly continued with occasional stops to far western Germany. It would stop once or twice a day at a train station in some small town. We would get off briefly to stretch our legs on the platform, and we were served mugs of soup from a huge pot by some of the town's people. Eventually we stopped outside Essen for a day. That night there was a huge bombing attack on the factories in Essen by American and British planes. We sat huddled in a damp ditch next to the railroad tracks, hoping the train would not be bombed. We shivered as we watched the Allies destroying Essen and its factories as waves of bombers droned past us overhead in the flare lit sky. Strangely, despite the fear, I remember finding the night sky magical when lit up by the flares that hung like small chandeliers against the vast black expanse overhead. The next day the train reversed and we once again continued back to Leipzig in eastern Germany. After two weeks on the train we finally disembarked in shock, exhausted, uncertain and fearful for our future. The second shock came when armed guards herded us into open trucks and took us to live in freezing cramped barracks in a German forced labor camp behind barbed wire.

In the camp my flag was a symbol that the authorities found offensive and so I secreted it under the straw mattress in my third level bunk bed in the small room that we shared with another family. We somehow survived that winter, the horrors of daily life in the camp and the meager kohlrabi or split pea soup rations with a piece of coarse bread. There were other kids in the camp and some of the older boys would like to tease, saying that the occasional lumps in the soup were parts of rats. But we were hungry and could not afford to fuss. Exhaustion marked the days for my parents and all other adults, who worked as slave labor twelve-hour

Ilga Winicov Harrington
Falmouth, ME

days in the adjacent factory. All children under the age of 14 faced school with daily terror in a one room school to learn German and some history. Our teacher was "Fräulein" with a wicked cane, which she loved to use on us at the slightest pretext by caning our outstretched hands or backs. There were no excuses or pretending to be sick back in the barracks.

We had a quiet and homesick Christmas by the light of one candle that winter, but then came spring and war caught up with us once again. When the advancing American forces opened the gates of the camp and freed us, we cheered and rejoiced. We brought out the flag, which once more could be openly displayed, with our unrealistic hopes of being able to return home. But that was not to be. In a short while we found that Leipzig was to be portioned off in the Russian Zone as the division of Germany proceeded after the end of the Second World War. It seemed to us incomprehensible, since the Americans had conquered that portion of Germany and now were giving it back to the Soviets. The Soviets were known for their severe retributions to all who had fled their regime. It was time to flee again and hope to reach the American Zone before the Soviets took over Leipzig.

"What did you do, Gram? Where did your family go?" asked Peter with baited-breath.

Gram just shook her head. "It was a scary time. My family and others in the camp worried and asked around for any means of transportation. The train lines were in shambles after the war and there was no transport to be had unless one had a lot of money, which of course we did not. But we were lucky," she continued.

We were fortunate, as five families using their combined last resources were able to barter the services of a truck and driver to take us west. We crammed everyone and our few remaining belongings in an open truck for our long journey. The rumors abounded of arbitrary check points, attacks on those fleeing west and confiscation of valuables by

Ilga Winicov Harrington
Falmouth, ME

unscrupulous individuals taking advantage of the chaos. The men in our group decided that my flag might give us an apparent official identity. Thus my flag was fastened to the front of the truck as our official symbol for transit and in a way guided us west.

We expected our trip to be uncomfortable in the open truck and it became even more so as we encountered a rainstorm and clogged roads slowing traffic to a crawl in many places. The roads were full of people fleeing west by whatever means possible, walking and dragging their belongings in small carts and even baby carriages. In those final chaotic days, before closing of the borders, it took us two days to finally reach Würzburg in the American zone, with incredibly slow traffic and trepidation about flat tires that might or might not be fixable.

In Würzburg our driver stopped in a rubble filled square and insisted on dropping us there in his hurry to return home before the borders were closed. I retrieved my now bedraggled flag from the hood of the truck while everyone unloaded their belongings. No one had any idea where we were, except despite everything we somehow felt safe.

Like most cities, Würzburg had suffered severely in the war, with bombed out bridges and much of the city in rubble. Our prospects looked dismal. A couple of the adults went in search of a rumored American Displaced Persons camp. We hung around near a huge pile of rubble where one of the men was rummaging for anything of value.

Suddenly, there was an ominous hiss and my stepfather pushed my mother and I down behind a high curb. I landed on my backpack with the flag and could see something shooting above us. In the quiet afterward I suddenly felt burning on my arm and elbow and a strange smell as the cloth sleeve of my dress was disintegrating. An unexploded phosphorus bomb had become disturbed by our friend and it caught us, despite the end of the war. It left spattered burn scars on my arm for years to come. My parents' pan-

Ilga Winicov Harrington
Falmouth, ME

icked search found a small house on a side street, where a reluctant German doctor treated my burns. His tall and hefty wife, wrapped in an enormous colorful apron stood near the door scowling as we left and muttered "vefluchte Ausländer." We found we had become undesirable foreigners.

After that excitement we eventually reached the Displaced Persons camp across the river Main, where we would live for the next five years. This was in a partially bombed out German military base that was converted by the United Nations into a camp to shelter refugees from WWII. It quickly became a community of 5000 Latvian refugees. The living conditions were crowded and meager with marginal food, but the amazing spirit of the people made it a real community.

Among the refugees were doctors and nurses who dealt with health issues. Teachers fashioned schools for children with the few books they had brought with them, and we were given thin blue notebooks provided by the UN Refugee Commission. We had both grade and high school, where most subjects were taught in Latvian, but we also had classes in German and English and for a while even in Latin. Performing artists devised entertainment in an old horse barn with a stage and rough benches fashioned from the partially destroyed buildings. There were concerts by individuals and choral groups. Refugee actors from theaters in Riga formed traveling companies to put on plays in many DP camps. It was amazing how stage decorations, props and costumes were created out of remaining rubble in the city and scraps from demolished buildings. Salvaged curtains were fashioned into fancy costumes and shiny jewelry was made from empty cans for plays set in history. We watched this make-believe world on the stage and forgot the drab everyday life in the camp.

All those years the flag lived on the family table, propped up in an empty can. In 1948, I carried it as the youngest singer in a procession at the 75th Anniversary United

Ilga Winicov Harrington
Falmouth, ME

Latvian Songfest. It was an incredible gathering of 17 choral groups from different DP camps in western Germany with 674 singers and more than 5000 people in the audience. Dressed in Latvian costumes we processed to the performance site on a hill outside Fischbach. There were risers on the hillside made from rough boards for the singers and the audience sat on grass. We sang all afternoon. It was an exciting and emotional day in my life.

"It must have been fun," added Peter.

"Oh, yes. I didn't even mind sleeping in a barn on hay the night before, since that was at least out of the chill night air and there was nothing else."

During those years in the American DP camp our living conditions were drab, we were poor, our food was basic and not very plentiful, but amazingly children could find joy and adventure even under such aberrant living conditions. Aside of school, to keep us youngsters out of trouble, there were Girl Scout and Boy Scout troops. Girl Scouts were a lot of fun. They got you outdoors and sometimes away from the camp. You learned to tie all kinds of knots, how to give first aid and use different codes. Best of all were the hikes and camping trips. We hiked for miles and miles all over the hills and through woods surrounding Würzburg. Sometimes in small groups we would follow a map and sometimes the leaders would set inconspicuous road markers, which we had to find in order to discover the proper route for an all-day hike covering miles among the terraced hillside vineyards.

Camping, like everything else, was primitive in those days. Six or eight of us girls would sleep in a large tent on some loose straw, each rolled in a blanket in a row like sardines in a can. After chilly nights we would wake up all bunched together for warmth. We would have straw sticking out of our hair as we would go to wash in the nearby river. Breakfast would be porridge cooked over an open fire. At our age, the fresh air and those miles of walking would ensure that there were never any leftovers in the pot, no matter how

Ilga Winicov Harrington
Falmouth, ME

inept the cook.

Often Girl and Boy Scout troops, camped within a short distance, would gather in one place for the evening entertainment. It would always take place round a huge bonfire with songs and skits. This invariably led to a "song-war" between the girls and the boys. Each group would make up unflattering words about the other to the tune of various folk songs. These "wars" would continue late into night until our leaders would finally chase everyone to their tents.

Sometimes different Scout troops would get together for a large campout with troops from other refugee camps and we would teach each other songs in Latvian, Lithuanian, Polish and Estonian. We were all young adolescents, all had seen a lot of tragedy in the last couple of years and presently could not think of a future. But we were out on a wonderful lark for those few days under a starry Bavarian sky.

Our last summer camp in 1949 was different and truly memorable in a castle built on hill near Rothenburg. It was a gleaming white structure on a hillside with nine levels, from several levels of cellars to the small turret on top. It had been abandoned by the army at the end of the war. In their wisdom, the refugee organization in charge of the American zone assigned it to serve as the basis for a month-long Girl Scout and Boy Scout camp for troops in the region. We put on our makeshift uniforms consisting of a skirt, blouse and a neckerchief, packed our backpacks, climbed aboard the open US army trucks and with our troop leaders went to live in a castle.

The girls had one floor and the boys had another floor. We slept on cots, ate in a common mess hall and took turns at kitchen duty. Most days we went on hikes, worked on our merit badges and played games during that wonderful summer. And there were evening assemblies held in a proper mirrored ballroom. The aged mirrors were less than pristine, but there was a piano and in the evenings we held dances. For an adolescent girl, head full of romantic notions, learning the

Ilga Winicov Harrington
Falmouth, ME

Viennese waltz in a mirrored ballroom was a dream come true, even if most of the boys found her too young to notice.

During those years in Würzburg, it became apparent that Realpolitik would never allow us to return home to Riga. The DP camps were to be closed and it was time to search for a new permanent home. We applied to emigrate to USA and thus began months of endless paperwork to document our identity, health and moral character. Finally, the flag and we boarded another ship to emigrate to the USA. We were sponsored by the Lutheran church with a six-month work guarantee for my parents. Since then, this flag has resided together with the American flag in several states. We came to a new country to embrace new customs and fashion our futures, but the past can never be forgotten.

"So, you see," Gram concluded, "this flag represents a unique and interesting story. That is why I saved it all those years."

"Wow Gram, no wonder the flag is so worn after all this time!"

Peter looked up to his grandmother, who only smiled softly and hugged him close.

Jean Lawrence
Waldoboro, ME

Ready to Celebrate

Two hundred years ago, as I was being formed,
some dedicated Waldoborough citizens were making plans
    for my home.
They chose a piece of land, one of the highest spots in the
    village
for their new house of worship.
Members purchased pews, and before the carpentry was
    complete,
free and clear of debt was the Old North Church.
To the spire of the church I came and was lifted up.
Here was my home and, given me by my Revere and Sons
    creators, my calling:
"The living to the church I call, And to the grave I summon
    all."

For 115 years, I encouraged villagers to Meeting House Hill
to behold the splendor of my home and to worship.
For years, the elite of the village entered through my doors
until time and dissention took their toll, and the
    congregation all but disappeared.
I was the silent witness as the church became abandoned.
In 1935, the few descendants of the original founders
    agreed to raze the building.
The pieces of what had once been a vibrant house of
    worship were distributed,
and the site and I were given to the town.

Jean Lawrence
Waldoboro, ME

Once again, plans were made for a new edifice;
a new high school was erected, and I was established on
      the roof.
Housed simply, my role was to call pupils to the school.
Education, not worship, was the new goal of my pealings.
I sent out my tones with joy. Students came and went for
      another 54 years.
Then, the school became outdated and crowded.
I'd always been a part of Meeting House Hill, and all of a
      sudden, I was homeless.
No one who knew me wanted to see me gone,
and yet a quandary arose: what should be done with me?

For a while, I was placed on a trailer, not a real home,
and hauled through town on parade days.
Some said I should be stored behind the Town Office
      Building;
others suggested, the Old Custom House.
I became not only a relic of Waldoboro's past, but also
      historically valuable,
while the haulers of my trailer grew older.
And so, in 1989, with the town's blessing, I found a new
      home at the historical society.

Now, here I hang, all 929 bronze pounds, in a splendid new
      housing
made by a local carpenter's hands from actual photos of my
      original enclosure.
I'm protected from the elements and rung on special
      occasions.
I'm ready for the bicentennial celebration of our state.
I'm ready for the next 200 years.
I am Waldoboro's Revere Bell.

Jeanine Stevens
Sacramento, CA

Dog Days

Heat! Chiggers!
swimming holes all gone algae,
"In bloom," we say.
Feet calloused from hot sidewalks,
skin still peeling.
Will last year's shoes fit?
Days like old parchment,
nights slumber long—slow turning of colors.
Smart dogs lie in shade
or crawl under the porch, occasionally
get up for a lap of water.

Last chance for vacation: Northern Minnesota,
large chunks of great Pike
sealed in dry ice, early Chippewa Pow Pow?
Time over for visiting country cousins,
farm boys naked under overhauls,
fat "Moon Pies" from the corner store.
Sunflowers and hollyhocks go to seed.
Topaz fireflies disappear.

I look forward to dry fields, walking
through corn stalks, fibers rattling shoulders.
Air out the Hudson Bay blankets!
(By January, so cold we won't notice scratchy wool.)
Soon the Frosty Freeze will close for the season.
Have the beans been put by?
Pull boots from storage;
put a Sears Catalogue in the outhouse!
Mother says, "Time to come in."

Marilyn Weymouth Seguin
Akron, OH

Loon Lyrics

*This of the loon—I do not mean its laugh, but its looning—
is a long-drawn call, as it were, sometimes singularly human
to my ear,—hoo-hoo-ooooo, like the hallooing of a man on a
very high key, having thrown his voice into his head. I have
heard a sound exactly like it when breathing heavily through
my own nostrils, half awake at ten at night, suggesting my
affinity to the loon; as if its language were but a dialect of my
own after all.*

—Henry David Thoreau

One of my earliest memories is listening to the sound of
a loon at my parents' lakeside cabin. If only I could write
that sound in words, but you can't spell a tremolo. Thoreau
tried but he didn't even come close. If you have a computer
with an internet connection, you can summon the sound of
the loon. This water bird makes four distinct sounds—and
some believe each sound is associated with its own message.

Many writers have celebrated the loon in literature,
including poets Hamlin Garland and Kathleen White, and fic-
tion writer Margaret Laurence. The loon is a beautiful crea-
ture to behold, even from a distance. The ruby red eyes help
its underwater vision, for the loon is a diving bird that makes
its main diet of fish. Its head is dark green, a striking con-
trast to its pure white breast and necklace of white stripes.
Ojibwa legend says that the loon got its necklace from a man
in return for the gift of the man's sight.

But it is the sounds that loons make that single them out
from other water birds. The Chippewa believed the cry of the
loon was the omen of death. Maybe that is why TV viewers
often hear loon soundtracks during scary scenes. Their
haunting cries and melodic tremolos are heart stopping,
especially when heard in the evenings or late at night.

Marilyn Weymouth Seguin
Akron, OH

One evening at the end of a summer, I sat in the twilight with my husband, my sister and brother-in-law on our Maine cabin deck. Very close to shore, a loon broke the surface of the water, and then seeming to stand on its tail, flapped its powerful wings and displayed its magnificent black and white plumage, but remained in the water. The bird then lifted its slender beak to the sky and cried. In the distance, another loon, perhaps the mate of the loon we had been watching, replied. We didn't know it at the time, but that was the last time we would sit together by the shore listening together to the sound of the loon. In just a few weeks, my brother-in-law would die at home of a heart attack at the age of 50.

No one who has heard a loon cry will ever forget it. It's as though the sound comes from a spirit between this world and another place—not quite of that other place, but trying to get from there to this side. Perhaps the sound is a gift to those of us in the world who will one day cross to that other side.

***

Sylvia Little-Sweat
Wingate, NC

PANDEMIC

Pandemic fears go viral—worldwide.
All humanity is at risk or victimized.
No ventilator stops this viral stealth.
Distressed breath precludes death.
Emergency Rooms are battle zones.
Masked—it invades Nursing Homes.
Infections terrorize and millions die.
COVID-19 offers no *Quid Pro Quos.*

Marcia Annenberg
ME & NY

Lock-Jaw

They spent their lives
    Sparring
thrust and blow
a continual flow
  of domination and retreat
subservient to an idea
  of being faithful
  to an expectation
  in itself an illusion

The staying on
  despite the daily torture
defeated in each other's eyes
  having only the other to despise
increased the bondage

What could have been worse
  perhaps
was having nothing to be disappointed in
  having nought
  except themselves
  and the great world beyond
    which only brought
    questions and unknowns
    into the mind
    and gave no comfort
      but only served
      to set the locks
       into a deeper mold
       beyond which neither one
       would choose to grow.

Karen E. Wagner
Hudson, MA

Unresolved

I forage in vain
for his headstone,
the place where I can
lay flowers on his birthday.
But he left no touchstone
for me, no mossy slab
of granite with wheat grass
growing over it,
his name engraved boldly
followed by birthday
in smaller font,
then date of death
and maybe a short message
like "He rests with the angels."
And I would lay violets
upon that stone to say
"I was here and thought of you."
Perhaps then he would be reminded
of me too, draw solace
from the memories.

His choice
to have his remains
flung over the abyss
takes away my anchor,
leaves me adrift
with no place
to lay my flowers
or shed my tears.

Warren D. Southworth, Sr.
Searsport, ME

Trees

The tree I bend to send the other tree
To do my will and kill the deer,
Or swell my heart
To see how close it will obey,
Or only serve to please my eyes
To watch one slender wood in arc,
The other on its way,
And speak to me of who I am
To even want to bend it,
Has died for me.

I honor death—
Of all trees which seed,
Grow to serve my need—
As I do the lives of those who went before,
Who, by their word and deed,
Have taught me how to use them.

***

Sally Belenardo
Branford, CT

Blue and White

New England's summer
color scheme is blue and white:
hydrangeas, fences,

fair skies, calm harbors,
Queen Anne's lace, chicory, clouds,
cottages, sailboats.

Mary Ann Bedwell
Grants, NM

Aphelion*

You said I was the moon and stars,
The sunshine in your skies.
You told me the light would never fade
But be reflected in your eyes.

You held me closely in your arms,
As you orbited round the light;
However you might circle round,
You kept me in your sight.

But time went by, as time will do,
And all things passed away.
The light is gone from your eyes
As you look at me today

But I understand, perhaps more than you
That the light isn't really gone.
We've simply changed positions—
You are now at aphelion.

*Aphelion—the point in the earth's orbit when it is at the farthest
distance from the sun

Cathy Koger
South Portland, ME

Tinker's Acre

Tinker Prinderville turned ninety-four October the thirtieth, 1964. At sunup, the screen door slapped behind her as she went out on her porch and viewed her yard, a lumpy carpet of acorns and burnt-red oak leaves. The scent of pine was in the Georgia air. Tinker's white tufts of hair shot out in all directions. She teetered, diminished inside her housedress. Her green eyes strained through their clouds; a tilt of her head to the left seemed to help. Her feet were bare and cold, her toenails thick, yellowed, and curled like a dog's. Tinker's skeleton was brittle and bent now, as was her house, whose weathered shingles, in a good wind, clicked against walls that had begun whispering Tinker's name.

She recalled a long-ago winter of unusual cold, when her kerosene stove had been empty. The woman from the County had come and found her in a spot of kitchen floor sun, rolled up in an unclean braided rug. Tinker cussed the tall, tight-lipped woman out the front door. It was that twilight that she first heard her name whispered repeatedly. She traced the voice to a spot of wall behind the taped color picture of Harry S. Truman and ripped at the president's nostrils and eyeballs in a fit of temper.

Longleaf pines stood sentry to the paint-bare house, and in the pine branches, the mockingbird sang its medley of titmouse, blue jay, kingbird, and toad.

"That ugly girl will come today," she announced to the mockingbird, "said it's my birthday." She strained for a reply.

Travelling through the wooded morning distance, voices reached her on the porch.

"It's the Cubans. Spying on me from over yonder," she announced loudly. "I'll shoot you by God if you step foot on my porch!" She cussed the vocal clutter in her head. What was to be done.

Cathy Koger
South Portland, ME

In the kitchen, Tinker fought with a box of tin foil. She managed a long sheet and, wobbling on tiptoes, almost reached the top of her bedroom door, got it up. She taped up several sheets until the door was mostly covered. "That'll keep them out." She sat, covering her ears and humming madly.

***

Midmorning, Tinker's niece, Lillian Turley, came for a visit from an hour's drive away across the Florida state line. She approached timidly, biting a fingernail as she walked from her Buick over the acorns to the front porch.

"Aunt Tink!" she called from the bottom porch step then cleared her throat. Lillian was short and struggled with her weight. Her head was crowned with heavily sprayed, mouse-gray curls. A gift-wrapped box of sweets was tucked under an arm. She drank hurriedly from the can of Tab she had brought with her.

Tinker appeared at the screen door, squinting at her niece. Lillian wondered if her aunt thought she was the long-expected CIA agent, the one she said had inserted the host of atomic rays in her six yellow teeth for storage. The can of Tab caught a spot of sun on its red aluminum. Lillian watched Tinker's face closely, relieved when it seemed she recognized the can of Tab.

"Yes, sweetie, it's me, Lillian. Today's your special day..." Tinker turned away.

"Don't step on my acorns."

Lillian fought useless tears. She regarded the bent back of her aunt with disgust. Her father's old stories—the intractability, the shootings, Lillian's grown daughter Theresa's embarrassment—"It's a thankless thing to do Mother. Just have her put in the State Hospital."

"Let's sit inside," Lillian said loudly. She waved off a little swarm of gnats to protect her face powder. Sometimes they'd

Cathy Koger
South Portland, ME

get stuck on her cheeks and neck.

They sat across from each other in the front room. Tinker rocked, and opened her present, a box of chocolate covered cherries. Lillian regarded the tin-foiled door from the corner of an eye, but could not bring herself to ask. She sat with her legs crossed at the knees, her skirt pulled neatly over her kneecap. Tinker smoked and ate the chocolate-covered cherries from the box in her lap. The pink liquid centers escaped at the corners of her mouth. "Look at that," Lillian thought. "Running right out her mouth. Damn." Lillian sat stiffly, her lips pressed into a thin line. Averting her eyes, she looked about the room at the faded floral wallpaper curled at its corners, and, here and there, gray stains.

Tinker had eaten all the chocolate-covered cherries and Lillian said, under her breath, "How you do that and stay so skinny I'll never know." She rose and handed Tinker a napkin.

"I'm going on now to the Winn-Dixie and get your groceries."

**

Tinker wiped her mouth, and the empty box of chocolates fell from her lap onto the floor, the paper wrappers scattering, quivering like moth wings. When the rumble of the departing Buick faded, Tinker came onto the porch to sit and mull over the day's work.

"It's the Cubans," she said out loud to her acre. "They want my pension. Then they give it to the Kremlin." The Cubans laughed inside her right ear. Tinker swatted at it as she would a mosquito. Her pension. She wondered where it came from. There was no recollection of a state office, of adding machines or brown Underwood typewriters, of lunch counters with slopped coffee. Tinker swatted twice at this most unnerving void of recollection for fear of tumbling into it.

Cathy Koger
South Portland, ME

***

Just after noon, the Buick returned and Lillian stepped gingerly among the acorns bearing the grocery bags, which she took into the kitchen. She heard Tinker in the back of the house. Lillian unpacked the groceries—cans of Vienna sausage and Deviled Ham, rolls of tin foil, white bread, Maxwell House Coffee, and milk. The milk man refused to deliver bottles to Tinker after she shot them from his hand three years ago. Tinker had been certain the milkman was a Russian assassin sent to poison her. The dairy manager had called Lillian to complain.

"Aunt Tink?" Lillian called as she put the groceries in the cupboards. She washed soiled pans, glasses, plates, and crusted forks, then cleaned the kitchen counter with Comet. She swept the crusty, discolored, linoleum floor.

"Aunt Tink? What are you doing? Let's have a birthday lunch."

Tinker appeared in the kitchen ready for her birthday in a sack of a blue dress. Her white hair was pushed back under a red knit cap. Her shoes were misshapen, holes cut in the sides for her bunions. Tinker said that she supposed her bunions were stabilizing protrusions, keeping her from tilting too far over to either side. Lillian pretended not to hear.

"Happy Birthday, sugar. I cleaned the kitchen for you, I know it's hard for you to keep this old house up. We should get you a maid once and for all."

Tinker grimaced and Lillian said, "Well nevermind that."

***

In her bright suburban brick house, Lillian kneaded ground beef and onions. Theresa handed her mother the snapped beans.

"Thank you, honey, just put them here."

Cathy Koger
South Portland, ME

Theresa, birdlike, leaned against the counter where her mother shaped a meatloaf.

"So how was the witch today? How old is she? A hundred yet?" She lit a cigarette.

Lillian put the log of meat into a pan.

"I wish you would quit those cigarettes."

Theresa blew her smoke away from her mother. "I'd say her mind went crazy a long time ago. And her brother. I never heard him say one word. When I was little I used to watch him in that rocker, staring at nothing. Creepy. How'd he die anyway?"

Lillian washed her hands. "I never knew. I told you before. No one would ever talk about it." She swept a can of Glade air freshener through the kitchen to spray away the smell of cigarette smoke. She thought to buy a can for Tinker's house.

***

Tired from her birthday, and the annoying visit from her niece, Tinker poured a cup of old morning coffee. Sloshing a trail onto the porch, she heard a new voice in her head, a Russian man announcing incoming laser beams. Tinker jumped at the stabbing of her scalp. When it was over, she lifted a hand slowly to feel the laser's entry points, the constellation of piercings.

The laser stabbings came again at dusk and stayed long into Tinker's night. Through her television shows, her bath, her tin-foiled door, resting in the moonlight on her bed quilt.

In the early morning, Tinker's fingertips with their thick, claws carefully touched each scab. She shakily lit the last cigarette from the crinkled pack. When she finally rose to tend the garden of voices, she strained her eyes through the oaks and pines in the direction of the near stagnant creek, its banks a frenzy of green flies. On the other side sat the colored shanties, where the Cubans now were sheltered, spying

Cathy Koger
South Portland, ME

on her.

Once in the bygone days she'd shot at them, at their flee-ing backs in the trees. The shot from her dead brother's twenty gauge shotgun had punched holes into a pine, there still, bark grown around as skin wrapping a new wound.

Tinker rummaged through the kitchen cupboards, find-ing her favorite, Vienna Sausage.

"Miz Prinderville, eat the Vienna Sausage," commanded the one who wanted her pension checks. Tinker obeyed hes-itantly, then put the empty can down in her lap. She sat at her stove in a straight-back chair, eyes fixed on the small can. "I'm going to die," she spoke out loud. "Murdered by poi-soned Viennas." She waited for a vomiting and thrashing death, confused when it did not come.

The flattening sun lit Tinker and the empty can in her lap. The gentle light combed her white weedy hair, careful of the scabs from the rays, glassened her green eyes, then painted yellow the drape of skin from her neck, the twigs of collarbone. Tinker moved her thin lips, arranging the voices' threats from worse to most worse.

The sun went down and left Tinker in the cacophony of demands, name-calling, and vile cussing directed at her most private crevices of body. At her bony buttocks and hanging, vacant bosom. She raised fists of knotted knuckles and pressed them to her head.

The shotgun leaned against a wall in the kitchen corner. Tinker pressed up from the straight-back chair and grabbed it. One voice landed in front of Tinker. She fired, and the shot sent splinters of kitchen chair about Tinker's bare feet. She put the gun away but she felt a chill step through her bones. Life would leave her through the top of her patchy head if something wasn't done. In the kitchen she saw it. The rolls of tin foil.

Morning arrived with birds and lofty clouds in a pale sky. Tinker sat still in her rocker on the porch. She had a grimy pink housecoat on and no slippers. The morning was cool

Cathy Koger
South Portland, ME

and a wind whipped fallen leaves about the ground. Upon Tinker's head was her red knit cap adorned with lint, and under the cap, corners of tin foil stuck out above white shoots of her hair. She spoke to her acre.

"Where is that ugly fat girl. I need more tin foil! Lots more. They get through it after a time."

She leaned forward, glancing sharply about her, and whispered loudly. "Don't say that so damn loud. They get on to this and next time that girl prisses up my steps with them grocery bags I won't have a head left at all. Idiot girl." Tinker looked away stiffly to her pines. "Have to change that foil every hour." And her eyes filled.

She started a frantic rocking. After a time she walked about her acre, not too far astray. Worrying, worrying about the coming nightfall. They were all out there in her piney woods, hiding, laughing. Each and every tree had a Cuban behind it. There would never be reprieve without more tin foil. Tinker would not call her niece on the telephone for help as the Cubans always listened in.

Upon the rising of a yellow moon that twilight, Tinker was at her stove, warming and worrying. Should she lay down in her bed, the foil would slip off and the rays were waiting for just such an opportunity. So she sat up to sleep, but because of her God-given forward angle, the cap and tin foil slipped off into her lap as she slept. In the dawn she cried, daybreak illuminating her lap, the crinkled sheet of foil and the little red cap.

***

Lillian squirmed in her chair at the bridge table, holding her clubs and diamonds close, pondering her bid. The tally card next to her sweating glass of sweet tea marked the afternoon's passing, the murmurs and complaints of her friends in the foursome, the wafts of smoke from Old Golds, the Tomato Aspic vibrating on the four luncheon plates.

Cathy Koger
South Portland, ME

"So," prodded Violet, who frequently boasted of the longevity of a friendship begun forty some years earlier at Jackson High, "Missus Pokey, can you manage a bid, or do we have to wait 'til Hell freezes?"

Lillian narrowed her eyes and met the question at last with a competent bid.

"Two clubs and if y'all had an old crazy blood aunt like I do —"

"Oh my, not that ol' coot again," said Gladys, pale in the face from her recent cancer. "She still alive?"

Violet put her cards down and lit a cigarette. "Lillian, I'm coming up there with you to that house and see what the hell's going on. First thing tomorrow. She can't be as awful as you say or she'd be dead out there all by herself. People like that just don't live long out in the country. She'll freeze to death soon as it turns colder."

The ladies finished their hand then moved into Lillian's back yard to inspect the beauty of her azalea bushes.

"Vi, if we even set foot on that rotten porch, she'll shoot us. She don't know you anymore." Lillian tried to flick an ant from a petal. "No telling what she's likely to do."

After her friends drove away, Lillian got out the Glade.

***

The mockingbird landed in the morning mist on the electric wire that attached Tinker Prinderville's dying house with the pine pole that took the world to the old woman and received nothing in return. The thickly wrapped black wire sagged as the old house leaned toward the pole. Little talons gripped the wire and Tinker sensed on the breeze a thing, foreign, and full of intent.

"The agents," she groaned. "With guns this time." She caught sight of the bird's sway on her wire. The bird made loud announcements, seeming to side with the agents. Tinker pressed out her cigarette, adjusted the foil under her

Cathy Koger
South Portland, ME

knit cap, retrieved the shotgun, and crept down the porch stairs, holding on tightly to the rail. Then under the electric wire she stopped and strained to look up at the bird and raised her shotgun. The impossible angle on her bowed frame and heavy lift of the gun sent Tinker backwards onto a bed of acorns, pine needles, red ants, and green florescent beetles.

Tinker's vertebrae snapped like twigs. The mockingbird heard and tilted its head to give Tinker an eye, which she met, though briefly. The sky above Tinker, with its stain of bird, was erased.

***

Heavy charcoal clouds hung low over the pinelands passing by out of the Buick's windows as Lillian drove over the state line. Violet sat beside her eating a Three Musketeers candy bar and drinking from a thermos of hot coffee, pleased that she had talked Lillian into bringing her along. The air teemed with the approach of rain.

Lillian glanced at the pastel concrete block motels, the roadside stands with their yellow signs every one hundred yards on a countdown to zero. Cherry Bombs. Country Cured Ham. Pecans.

Tinker's acre began on the east side of the cracked and weedy two-lane road with a handsome stand of loblolly pine and spits of tickseed and fleabane. At the turn to the house the mailbox had long fallen over and lay in decay. The Buick crept up the dirt drive.

Lillian and Violet found Tinker on the ground. They slowly circled her, hands covering their mouths, eyes wide. Violet shooed the flies floating about Tinker's face. Lillian knelt to feel a pulse with shaking fingers but found only still, hard bone. She gagged at the sight of her aunt Tinker who lay ashen in her dirty housedress, host to a gathering of industrious insects.

Cathy Koger
South Portland, ME

The house stood silent, porch empty, spiders weaving, curtains swaying in the open windows. On the ground between Tinker and her house lay her red cap, and a square of tin foil twitched on the ground, caught on a pine twig.

"Lillian, you stay with her. I'll call for the sheriff." Violet hurried to the house.

The house was dark inside, except for the glint from the door covered over with tin foil. Breezes swept in through the open windows and surrounded Violet with the faint tinkling of loose corners of foil. Nothing she saw was as she knew the world to be. Violet remembered to make the call to the sheriff department. "An old woman is dead in her yard," she reported. "I don't know how."

Lillian was kneeling in the pine needles by the body, crying quietly.

"Violet, look." Lillian pointed to Tinker's hands which were balled into fists, stuck fast in her final great temper.

The sheriff's car was heard coming up to the house over the acorns.

Violet looked at Lillian and her swollen eyes. "Good Lord, Lillian. You just never know do you."

Tinker lay broken in the pine needles. The Cubans departed on the wind. Then came a rain, soft and kind.

Craig Sipe
Orr's Island, ME

Bagged

potato chip morsels
intense slippery
sour cream smidgens
salty bottom
bag dregs
why should a poem
at midnight
exist
about them
those savory
iambic iotas
sliding from
a finger's tweeze
counting both
as sustenance
and sin

***

Steve Troyanovich
Florence, NJ

garden of yesterday's dreams

like a mirror
        rusty with memories

—Abdellatif Laabi

still the moonlight nectar
in translucent sorrow
time's lost garden
blooms in starless shudder

Gina Montini Mosca
Augusta, ME

The Five and Dime

Two vagabonds
wandering Downtown
My sister and I
Tramping among the hustle-and bustle
Christmas bells ringing
snow crunching
cold vapor rising
from our mouths and nostrils
Mismatched mittens
and hand-me-down coats
Swimming in oversized boots
The look of hunger or fright in our eyes
Echoes of arguing and yelling
ringing in our heads

The merriment of shoppers
familiar Christmas music
and storefront displays
are a welcome distraction
We curiously peer through
frosty window panes
"You two must be freezing"
a jolly elderly woman says
startling us in our tracks
She is overburdened with gift bags
Pure white hair, rosy cheeks
and a sleek red woolen coat
She sort of looks like Mrs. Claus
"Come in and have a warm drink!" she sings
Her eyes glisten, her warmth appealing
Blank distrustful stares follow
"Don't be afraid, come out of the cold"

Gina Montini Mosca
Augusta, ME

We follow her into the Five and Dime
and sit on the stools at the counter
This place is familiar but has never
been experienced from the inside
"We'll have three hot chocolates!"
A lady in a gray dress and a white apron
balances a tray over her shoulder with
three mugs filled with brown liquid
topped with white clouds
She places the mugs in front of us
and we are intrigued

"Do you like whipped cream?"
We look bewildered
Is whipped cream white and fluffy?
Is it creamy and sweet?
Then we most surely will like it!
Chocolate milk-heated....how interesting
I bring the cup to my lips and imagine myself
swimming in a white cloud
The sweet fluffy cream is a wonderment
to my tongue and taste buds
I think this tastes like ....happiness
The steamy liquid chocolate trickles
down my throat into my chest
and I feel warm and peaceful inside
I think this feels like...............love
The stress and worry melts away
This lady and this place
feel loving and safe

"How much will this cost us?"
the nice lady chants
Our faces wince with worry
We haven't any money

(continued)

Gina Montini Mosca
Augusta, ME

"Don't worry it's my treat"
she lovingly reassures us
"We pop a balloon for our price"
The lady in the gray dress brings
a bouquet of colorful helium balloons
over to the counter "pick one!"
I pick the pink one
"Go ahead, pop it with this pin"
I jab the pink balloon
As it explodes
a small paper
drops to the ground
which reads five cents
The elderly lady cheers
Sister pops a light blue balloon
and her paper reads ten cents
"Well done" the sweet old lady says
"Mine is full price, 25 cents!"

She reaches inside her pocketbook
and rummages for her coin purse buried
beneath her rain hat and handkerchief
The aroma of spearmint gum seeps out of her
clutch and invades my nostrils
She takes three coins from her beaded purse
and places a nickel in my hand
Her face is glowing with happiness
She gives Sister a dime
We proudly give our money to the
lady in the gray dress

"Now hurry home before it gets dark"
the kind old lady tells us
Her warmth has touched us
and our stone bodies soften

(continued)

Gina Montini Mosca
Augusta, ME

enough to accept a hug
We thank her and scurry away
but turn around and
blow her a kiss
She waves goodbye
looking more radiant.........than before
All of our hearts expanded...........a little more
Peace is found,
Love is abound
Downtown
At the Five and Dime

***

Minal Mineva Patel
Portland, ME

The Couch

Sitting down for a minute
Won't hurt,
Will it?

Lying down for a minute
Won't hurt,
Will it?

Closing my eyes for a minute
Won't hurt,
Will it?

I think
I've got work to do.

ZZZZZZZ.......

Austin Gallant
Rockport, ME

Eventide

The hum of continuation,
a crescent skulks,
imperfections blanket the scheme.

A moment in time,
still yet stirring,
isolated and abashed.

We turn,
up,
abroad.

The lone star glimmers,
promising guidance,
cloaking its deceptions.

Imperfections no longer stagnant,
impeding differently every moment,
nonetheless exact and unaltered.

Leaves droop,
needles sink,
color weakens.

Imperfections reappear,
frequently erased,
by familiar darkness.

A maternal spirit,
the failsafe cure,
a reliable comfort.

Monica Cane
Ripon, CA

The Rearranged Nest

Writing is healing for me because it reminds me where I was and where I am. I wrote the following seven months ago and can honestly say God has walked me through the strong emotions I was feeling at the time and continually helps me to adjust and have joy in my rearranged nest.

Fifty-five days ago the last of my three children left home, transferring to a college three hundred and fifty-two miles away. Although I communicate with one if not all of my three children via text, phone or Face-time on a regular basis, I am keenly aware that my nest is now empty.

The unsolicited advice I have been receiving since my nest has changed has been, *this is your time, so enjoy it.* What I believe these well-meaning people are saying is that the empty nest season is a time to rediscover the things that I enjoy that I hadn't been able to focus on over the past few decades of raising children.

I am sure there was nothing but goodness meant by such advice but the truth is, I spent the past few decades focusing all of my energy on exactly what I wanted to focus on, my family.

My nest was something I always wanted. I never gave up personal dreams to have it. I didn't tuck aside a bucket list of desires until my kids grew up, the nest was my main desire. I did pursue other desires of my heart while raising them, such as writing, speaking and serving God in various ways but ultimately having my full nest and raising my baby birds was my dream.

So here I am, letting go, while staying near, and adjusting to the feel of my new nest.

Of all the different adjustments I have made in the last fifty-five days, to my complete surprise, food shopping has been the absolute worst. Who knew pushing a cart down the

Monica Cane
Ripon, CA

bread and crackers aisle could bring on a mad rush of anxiety and cause me to hyper-ventilate, but it does.

I spent years on that bread and crackers aisle picking up jars of peanut butter, whole wheat bread, Ritz Crackers, Fig Newtons, graham crackers and other crackery-snacks my kids loved, all from that one section of the store. But as of fifty-five days ago it's just my husband and I, it was a rude awakening to realize that we needed very little from that aisle.

And so we are trying to adjust.

In less than sixty days I've learned just how pro-active one needs to be when re-arranging their nest. Since realizing the bread and cracker aisle is now my nemesis, I've decided to by-pass it all together. For now, I've signed up for a pre-made meal service and changed grocery stores for the little things I need. I hid the snack basket that my kids would put their snacks in for years, and also hid familiar cups that they still actually use when they come to visit.

I've had to do a lot of odd re-arranging in order to shift my strong mama emotions of wanting my nest full again, instead of allowing my baby birds to fly. In truth they are not flying so far that they don't know where the nest is, it's just I prefer to have them in it. But it's time to shift.

Shifting is not easy but it is how we all become who we are meant to be in different seasons of our lives. So if in this empty nest season I have to oddly re-arrange a few things, it's okay. Sometimes a little rearranging helps us all to fly a little bit better.

Robert B. Moreland
Pleasant Prairie, WI

Go the Distance

Sometimes in quiet recesses
of my mind, I hear the still voice
of God as He romances my heart
with those dreams I dare to touch, reach.

For He longs for me to know those
good and endearing qualities
that, made in His image, make me like
Him; Abba, Father; Holy God.

How could I understand what a
Father is, mine distant, failing
to connect that one sacred bond!
Caught unaware, saw Field of Dreams.

Why is it every time I watch
Ray finally meet his dad, "Catch
a good game" and introduces his
family, I begin to choke up?

"Is it heaven?" "No, Iowa."
Why is it that as we see, and tears
form in the corner of our manly eyes;
"Would you like to have a catch, Dad?"

Perhaps as the French horns echo
and the credits roll, we all feel
His pain, go the distance and hope
that if we build it, He will come.

Rosemary Sedgwick
Boxborough, MA

Rest in Peace

Standing at the kitchen sink,
noticing the shed petals
of a small blossom
picked yesterday
for the windowsill vase,
I understand at last
that graveside comfort,
"Rest in Peace."

It is not hard to pick a flower.
It is that the day after
you have salvaged three tiny roses
from the drought-stricken garden,
one is already gone.

I understand;
even the flowers,
—especially the flowers—
allow you no peace.

***

P. C. Moorehead
North Lake, WI

Again

A stream, from its source
In mountains far, reaches sand
to renew anew.

E. H. Gerard
Penobscot, ME

Death's Registry

Some beg to die
But death, overworked,
Is bored with their cries.
"Wait your turn," he smirks.

No skipping in or pushing through
Red tape and procedure
Are the rule—Or
You don't meet the leader.

The old grow impatient in the line
Women chat with a neighbor,
Men look behind.
Children jostle, a few tremble.

At last, emaciated, eyes blank
The beggar passes his papers,
Waits to slip through the gate.
"Sorry, can't accept this waiver.
Next."

***

Genie Dailey
Jefferson, ME

Sprinkles

Droplets fly, sprinkling
Me, and creating rainbows.
Wet puppy shaking.

Kate Kearns
Scarborough, ME

Night Poem for an Anxious Child

The trees are awake—you are
never alone. Their leaves
scatter the rain into mist

to help the impatient ground
soak in every familiar morsel.
The cricket's stridulations

are not strings, but percussion,
tiny wings on a belly drum.
You'll hear spring coming

in their tempo—slow for cold
and faster with the heat.
The atoms in a cricket's wing

dance the same rumba
as the atoms in your eyelashes.
You are made of them, I

am made of them, too,
and everything you're afraid of,
even the ones you can't name,

even the stars, are crafted
from the same infinite materials.
Starlamps started their way

to your sky lifetimes ago. New lights
are setting out across the cosmos
all the time. The dark is temporary.

Juliana L'Heureux
Topsham, ME

Finding Michelangelo in Bruges

My girlfriend and I walked all over the medieval city of Bruges to find the beautiful Madonna and Child, also known as Our Lady of Bruges, by the Italian sculptor Michelangelo. I was visiting my American friend who was working in Brussels, Belgium at the time. We decided to take the train to Bruges, where I was determined to find the Madonna of Bruges. Surely, there would be lines to enter the location, so we assumed the sculpture would be easy to find, if we just looked for the crowds. Well, we never found the famous sculpture. Although, we knew it was located in The Church of Our Lady of Bruges, we tried, but couldn't find it. In fact, we walked in and out of about a half dozen of Bruges' Catholic churches, without a hint as to where the Michelangelo sculpture would be on display.

It's difficult to understand how we missed finding the church where she is located in Bruges. Nevertheless, we wandered through the beautiful and pristine city's medieval streets without ever finding the church where the Michelangelo sculpture was displayed.

But, I didn't give up.

Frankly, for anyone who has enjoyed the opportunity to visit the historic city of Bruges, it's probably difficult to understand how I could have missed finding the Church of Our Lady of Bruges. Still, there were no directional signs to the church that has a history, dating to the 13th, 14th and 15th centuries, with an address being 800 Mariastraat. Obviously our excursion to find the church was focused in the wrong direction.

Nonetheless, our determination presented us with a reason to immerse ourselves in the city's antique charm. We roamed from one street to the next and enjoyed every church we visited, because each one seemed like a special museum.

Juliana L'Heureux
Topsham, ME

Indeed, the Flemish art and late-gothic architecture are fascinating finds, located in nearly every nook and cranny lining the city's narrow streets. Likewise, the municipal buildings and church architectures are interesting. Although Bruges has a history as ancient as when the Vikings once occupied the area, there has fortunately been little destruction caused by the wars that ravaged Europe. Even the two European wars in the 20th century did not diminish the buildings or cause structural harms. Thank goodness, Bruges was somehow spared, because any ravaging would almost certainly have caused the Michelangelo Lady of Bruges sculpture to be damaged. Instead, she and the church have survived intact, for centuries.

Michelangelo created the beautiful Madonna of Bruges in 1504. She is not a large sculpture. When compared to the impressive size of Michelangelo's other classics like, for example, the stunning Pieta in the Vatican's St. Peter's Basilica, or the Moses located in the St. Peter's in Chains in Rome and David in the Galleria dell'Accademia, in Florence, she is serene and exquisitely modest. Michelangelo sculpted her from a single piece of marble. She measures 4 feet 2.5 inches tall, because she was likely designed to be placed on a church altar, which is where I eventually found her. Albeit, it took a second visit to Bruges, to accomplish the goal.

About two years after my first visit, my husband and I returned to Belgium to again visit with my friend, who was still living in Brussels. We took the train to Bruges where, all over again, I began my quest to find the Madonna of Bruges. Our visit was during November, when the daylight hours were short, so it was important to find the statue before sunset. We walked up and down nearly every street, circling the city's well-known central fish market, knowing we were traveling in circles. Dusk was approaching; there wasn't much time to find the statue during daylight hours. It so happened, there was an outdoor postcard kiosk displayed on the steps of a gift shop. Since I am a post-card accumulator, I decided

Juliana L'Heureux
Topsham, ME

to look through the displayed cards. That was when I found a postcard with the picture of the Michelangelo Madonna printed in English. The inscription even gave me the name of the church we should have been looking for, but the time was getting late, so it seemed futile to try to find her. Therefore, I purchased the card while telling my husband, "Well, this is obviously as close as we are going to get to the Madonna of Bruges." Frustrated, I was about to give up and go back to Brussels, but not before purchasing something meaningful to take home. Instinctively, we knew this would be our last visit to charming Bruges. We saw a linen shop located across the street from the post card kiosk, so it was convenient to browse for a few minutes, and to appreciate the exquisite embroidered linen table cloths and colorful handiwork in the shop's window. In fact, we quickly ran inside and selected an embroidered table cloth to give as a Christmas gift. It turned out that the shop's proprietor was fluent in English. We started chatting about our visit to Bruges and that's when I happened to mention about how we were disappointed by having to leave the city without ever finding Michelangelo's Madonna of Bruges.

"Why?" he replied.

"Because," I answered. "We can't find the church where she is located!"

To which he again replied, "Why?"

"Don't you know it is that church across the street? In fact, you can see it from here!"

"What? Oh my! It's THAT church?"

"Yes!"

"But, can my husband and I get inside to see the Madonna?"

"Well, I think the church closes at 4 PM, so you should see it, if you hurry," he said.

Indeed, we hurried, our purchase in hand, but only to find the front door, a large medieval entry, was already bolted shut. "Oh no, we're so close but we can't get inside," I said

Juliana L'Heureux
Topsham, ME

in despair.

Just then, I saw a rather shadowy figure walking to the rear of the church. I immediately said, "Look, let's follow that person!"

My husband was skeptical. "I think the church is closed," he said.

Nonetheless, I took off with my husband on my heels, because I didn't want to lose sight of the person who was clearly going to enter the church from a rear door. I could not tell if the figure we were following was male or female. The person was wearing a long dark coat with a hat, therefore, I never determined if he was a priest or just a citizen who happened to know how to enter the church. Sure enough, there was an open door where the shadowy figure had entered. We found ourselves in s small dark foyer with a window that provided just enough light to show us how to climb up a wide set of stairs.

We lost sight of the figure we followed, but we ascended the steps leading to very dark sanctuary There were no lights except for one spotlight focused on a side alter where, "taaaa-ddaa!" there she was, the brightly lit Madonna of Bruges. She instantly captured our hearts with her stunning serenity.

There we were, face-to-face, up close with the Madonna of Bruges. There were no crowds of tourists. One solo young man with long curly dark blond hair tied with a scarf at the nape of his neck, was seemingly keeping vigil with the Madonna. He stood peacefully and still at the foot of the spotlight that was focused on the sculpture in the otherwise dark sanctuary. Possibly, he was a student, because he wore a back pack. Just three of us, we were nearly hypnotized by the presence of being with the Madonna of Bruges. No words were spoken.

Our nearly magnetic trance was finally interrupted after about ten minutes of being in awe of the Madonna, when out of the darkness came a bellowing voice, spoken in broken

English, by a man with a deep Flemish accent. He was broadcasting to us as though we were in a crowded Grand Place. He gave a very authoritative directive, spoken from an invisible loud speaker system. "Dis churchen et in closen!" said the reverberating heavily accented voice. "Leave! Dis churchen et in closen!" His voice could have awakened the dead.

We certainly wanted to obey the order, so we quickly looked to find the door that we had entered in, but it was already locked. How could we exit a "churchen et in closen?" That's when a ghoulish figure with neck-long dark hair appeared to us in the darkness. Perhaps, he could have been the willowy dark figure we followed into the back entry. He proceeded to open the sanctuary's front door, the one we found locked on our first attempt to enter the building. Almost instantaneously, as soon as we exited the church, the massive medieval front door was slammed shut and loudly bolted behind us. We had experienced our first and last visit with Our Lady of Bruges.

To this day, I cannot understand how, during two visits to Bruges, we missed finding the Michelangelo Madonna of Bruges, until serendipitously, we took the risk, and followed the directions provided by a shop keeper and the footsteps of a willowy dark figure, walking in the dusk. Yet, the experience is vividly etched in my memory, even though it happened more than 20 years ago.

Obviously, there is a travel moral to this true story. Tourists who are fortunate to visit Bruges today will undoubtedly have the good sense to follow their Global Positioning System, better known as a GPS. We now have the advantage of travel technology, rather than having to depend on stalking a strange dark figure, while closing time sets in at dusk, on the Church of Our Lady of Bruges.

Travel to beautiful European cities like Bruges could be difficult for future curious tourists, who may not have the opportunities to freely roam around in strange places.

Juliana L'Heureux
Topsham, ME

Perhaps, the freedom to travel will be restricted until the world can provide safety from risks of exposure to pandemics. Certainly, when that time eventually comes, when "normal" becomes normal again, Our Lady of Bruges will still be there, at 800 Mariastraat, just like she has been since the early 16th century.

***

Erin Covey-Smith
Freeport, ME

Glance

Light-stunned clouds skittering
in bursts of color—unfettered
glory dancing across the sky,
as the wind clears the rain with all
the autumnal aplomb it can muster—

Until finally the prismatic bacchanal
settles into a crimson sigh, welcoming
silence after noisy twilight.

The moon distills the brilliance
into the finest concentrated silver,
almost trembling with all the fire
it contains, in one hairline crescent.

While I, undeserving, toss occasional,
careless glances out the window—
glances which inevitably rebound
in flagrant, unending wonder.

Cordula Mathias
Trevett, ME

Ready

I am out of love
with my winter clothes

I am more than ready
for some pink
and some gold

I am ready for warmth
rather than cold

My heart aches
for color, my
body feels bold.

***

Hunting Season

There is quite
a bit of raking
going on in my life
as the days grow shorter:
raking leaves
raking out the fireplace
raking over the past.

Not exactly
A Rake's Progress
but donning
my orange fedora
gives me a rakish feeling.

John T. Hagan
Springboro, OH

Class Reunion

A glossy missive came today
To bring a message that did say,
"Come join us and we'll celebrate;
Shake hands with ev'ry old classmate;
Toast and cheer our alma mater,
Making rival schools our fodder.
We'll dance and revel through the night,
Then breakfast in the new day's light."
At first, I thought, how grand a deal
To see old mates and share a meal;
Quaff vintage wines and break warm bread
(With those who weren't already dead.)
My mind's eye did erase five years
And conjured memories of peers
Who showed up at our last big bash
And looked like re-cooked succotash.
The guys poured drinks down flaccid jowls.
The girls bemoaned their stubborn bowels.
With furrowed brows and balding pates,
The guys revealed their dental plates.
The girls whose shapes were once hour-glassed
Were now droop-chinned and bulbous-assed.
There stood our grand old running back
(In self-esteem ne'er did he lack)
Reliving his great glory year
That gained in glow with each cold beer.
And near him stood class president,
A proud McMansion resident,
And he was with our sweet prom queen
Who in rehab is sometimes seen.
The N.H.S. was there that night,

(continued)

John T. Hagan
Springboro, OH

Dressed to the nines and quite a sight.
One turned to me and smugly said,
"Aren't you that dim-bulbed dunderhead
Who was always on probation,
Ranked dead-last in class location?"
A quick rejoinder I did lob,
"And how's your bandit husband, Rob,
The guy who's made the news of late
For hawkin' bogus real estate?"
She gave to me her shoulders, cold
And turned to Nan with shoulders rolled,
"I never liked that blatherskite.
Why do we always him invite?"
From just about each tongue and lip
Came efforts of one-upmanship.
Proud Paula bragged on children, smart.
Fat Freddie brayed on new golf cart.
Faux Frances claimed she'd traveled far.
Crass Cranston bared his bladder scar.
Vain Velma sported finger rocks.
Shrewd Sanford crowed he'd killed in stocks.
Tanned Tina raved on chic beach digs.
Rube Randy squealed of twelve new pigs.
Saint Sondra said she'd saved six souls.
Lout Larry lauded sleek black Rolls.
Prof Peter puffed his Ph.D.
Glib Glenda traced her family tree.
Brash Bradley bellowed all night long.
Lewd Linda flashed her X.L. thong.
Dolt Darrell did his Elvis thing.
Coy Clara claimed she'd touched The King.
Cool Carlin cooed in slick hairpiece.
Bad Brenda brought young stud from Greece.
Crude Crawford's jokes amused a few.
Hale Helen hyped her diet, new.

(continued)

John T. Hagan
Springboro, OH

Gauche Gavin of his exes railed.
Round Rita's liposuction failed.
Plump Patrick plied his politics.
Mild Melva shared her Yoga tricks.
Lush Leonard proved he's still a souse.
Snob Susan strutted her fourth spouse.
Throughout the night we did our best
To promulgate our verve and zest,
But, in fact, quite sad and dismal,
We'd reached depths that were abysmal.
Had not sign declared our function,
We'd resembled New-Hip Junction.
So this fifth year, I shall not go
To hear the blather I well know.
I won't bear that bore Bill Bounder;
Tolerate rude Rita Rounder.
I'll save that fifty bucks, so dear
And buy myself a case of beer.

***

Rosemary Sedgwick
Boxborough, MA

Chasing off Squirrels

Cardinals on the ground
don't mind squirrels around.
Don't they see those creatures
have insolent features,
and will steal all the suet
if I allow them to do it?

Andrew C. Miller
Deer Isle, ME

Somewhere Down East

First published in *The River*, 4 May 2020

In the summer of 1957, when I was ten years old, my father rented a cabin near Milbridge, in Down East Maine. It was near the end of a peninsula, several hundred yards from the ocean and surrounded by spruce trees. The wood siding was a dull green and except for red trim, blended into the evergreen forest. The cabin had no electricity and one of my chores was to carry water for drinking and washing from a nearby well. The outhouse, a closet-sized wooden structure that enclosed a two-hole pit latrine, was a short distance away. My mother cooked on a kerosene stove indoors or on a stone fireplace outside. We read by lamplight, ate meals on stools fashioned from nail kegs, and all slept in a single bunkroom. Above the main room was a tiny loft where I used to play, accessible only by ladder. Several times my father purchased live lobsters from a fisherman hauling traps just offshore. I had never seen live lobsters, watched them cooked, or eaten one.

My father learned about the cabin from its owner, a botanist friend who worked at the Smithsonian Institution. We knew about its primitive condition before leaving home. Although truly roughing it, the experience was not that unusual for my parents. Both were born near the turn of the century and grew up in homes without running water or electricity. These privations were minor, more than made up for by the availability of fresh seafood, the stunning views of rocky coves, nearby islands, and endless mudflats. For me, lugging water by hand and using an outhouse wasn't that bothersome. And, at that age, I would have assumed that everything—the outhouse, the dimly lit remote cabin—would remain unchanged forever.

Our home was in Pittsburgh and my father plotted our 850-mile, three-day trip to Milbridge using paper maps. He

Andrew C. Miller
Deer Isle, ME

recorded major highway intersections on 3x5 cards that he flipped through as we drove. Packed into our 1953 Plymouth, we traveled east on the Pennsylvania turnpike, then north on the New York thruway. After weaving about on side roads, we continued east on the brand new, partially completed Mass Pike. South of Portland, we joined U.S. Route 1, then followed the coast north and east through dozens of small towns until we reached Milbridge.

Before that two-week vacation, I had no experience with tides and rocky coastlines, knew nothing of marine life or saltwater. Possibly this was part of my father's plan: to introduce a little brine into my veins. He woke me early on the first morning and together we strode down a narrow path to the ocean. The sky was clear, and the sun poured through the evergreen branches, spattering the ferns and reindeer moss with bright yellow. We clambered over boulders to reach the tidal zone, then slipped and slid over greasy mats of rockweed to the water's edge. Airbladders on the stems made satisfying pops under our weight. I knelt beside a shallow pool, barnacles cutting into my knees, and pulled out a gray-green sea urchin, one of a tightly packed cluster. Its nearly motionless spines left tiny indentations in my skin. Sea stars were everywhere, carpeting the pools, draped over exposed rocks like sleeping cats. From a crevice between two rocks, my father pulled one out larger than his hand. When he saw the envious look on my face, he tossed it my way. I had never held one and marveled at its cold crusty arms that barely moved. Everything I saw—the creatures exposed by low tide, the huge boulders littering the shoreline, massive expanses of rockweed and kelp—was more dramatic and diverse than anything I had ever seen along lakes, rivers, and sandy beaches in Pennsylvania. By comparison, freshwater habits were dull and uninteresting.

Fifty years would pass before I returned to that cabin or that section of the Maine coast. Part of the reason was distance. After leaving Pittsburgh, I never lived closer than

Andrew C. Miller
Deer Isle, ME

1,000 miles from Maine. But the real reason was a fear that the cabin would never look the way it did in 1957. I didn't want to return and see it flooded with incandescent light, hear the steady hum of an electric refrigerator, or the rhythmic churning of a washing machine or dishwasher.

***

In the late 1990s I met Kathryn, who lived in Tallahassee but also owned a house and property on Deer Isle, about 60 miles southwest of Milbridge. We had the same political inclinations, loved cats, reading, and the out of doors. And, of course, there was the Maine connection. We married, then a few years later, retired. I began to think about that cabin. Was it still there, and would it have changed after 50 years? And, since I was older, would it seem different, perhaps not as exciting as it was back then?

***

It was a cold and rainy November afternoon in 2007, and we were driving east on U.S. Route 1 toward Milbridge. From the start, Kathryn was uneasy about my ability to find the cabin. I had gotten my initial bearings from *The Maine Atlas and Gazetteer* but planned to rely mainly on memory. I was certain it was near the tip of a peninsula, about six miles south of Milbridge. We had to find a gravel road that turned south off U.S. Route 1 near town. Kathryn kept reminding me that I had a lousy sense of direction and hadn't been there in half a century. Her humor wasn't helped by the weather. The rain showed no sign of letting up, and a light fog had begun to settle, obscuring the road in front of us.

As we approached Milbridge, I spotted a secondary road that cut off to the right. Although it wasn't gravel, it looked familiar and headed south. "This is it," I said.

Kathryn kept quiet until we made the turn. "Amazing

Andrew C. Miller
Deer Isle, ME

that you remember this so well—and you were only ten years old!" She nudged my shoulder. I detected a hint of sarcasm in her voice. Fifty years ago I was probably absorbed in *Mad Magazine* and not paying much attention. I couldn't think of a snappy response and remained quiet. Better not to roil the waters, especially if we had to drive back into town for directions.

It didn't take long before houses, trailers, and stacks of lobster traps gave way to abandoned apple orchards and old fields. The road narrowed and the asphalt began to deteriorate. Kathryn grabbed *The Maine Atlas and Gazetteer* and began flipping through pages. I pressed on.

A few minutes later, the bumpy pavement deteriorated to even bumpier gravel. The road narrowed and the power lines quit. The rest of the peninsula was off the grid. The lack of electricity was a key to my memory—this had to be the correct road. I spotted a weedy two-track lane that cut off to the east. It was narrow and quickly disappeared into the trees. We turned in, then stopped. The way forward was blocked by an old car.

"Probably a clammer," Kathryn said. "Bet he's got a gun."

I knew that clammers could be very suspicious of strangers snooping around their favorite spots. But hey, I wanted to find that cabin. Kathryn stayed in the car and I went ahead on foot.

***

A few hundred yards down the two-track road, I smelled wood smoke and spotted the cabin. A bit larger than I remembered, but still sheathed with green siding and red trim, surrounded by spruce trees. A young man was out front, hauling brush and feeding a fire. He didn't look like a clammer.

"Hello," I called through the trees. He stopped tossing branches into the flames and stared at me. He said nothing while I introduced myself and told him that my family had vacationed here in 1957. I explained that my father had known the owner. He tossed another branch in the fire, paused while the smoke rose, then motioned toward a strip of land near the ocean.

"That was my grandfather. He's buried over there."

The man was from Blue Hill, not far from Deer Isle, and had traveled up for the day to do chores. Quite a coincidence that we were both here at the same time.

The cabin had not been sold and was still in the family. Sometime during the sixties, they added a room on the first floor with a line of windows that faced east. The new ones matched the original windows—two small panes over a single. We went inside. The tiny loft where I used to play had been converted to a full-sized room. Nail kegs surrounded the table and the bunkroom was unchanged. They still fetched water from a well and there was no electricity, not even a generator. I saw one concession to modernity: a propane-fueled refrigerator, stove, and lights. But still no electricity to power a telephone or computer. A two-week stay today wouldn't differ much from one 50 years ago.

I've heard many warnings about returning to childhood haunts. They will seem smaller, less magical, more mundane when viewed through adult eyes. But for me, nothing had changed. I almost expected to see my father carrying wood to the fireplace or hear my mother calling us for supper. During our vacation in the fifties, my parents were about the same age as I was during this return visit. That made me feel a bit giddy. I pondered the difficulty of that trip for them, especially my mother. The burden of preparing meals, keeping bodies and clothes clean without hot water from the tap must have been tough. Something a ten-year old wouldn't worry about.

***

It was a sunny morning in 2018, and Kathryn and I were

Andrew C. Miller
Deer Isle, ME

again on Route 1 driving toward Milbridge. Ten years had elapsed since our previous visit, and much had happened. Both my children were married and had children of their own. I had been thinking more about the cabin, and worried that it might have been sold or knocked down. If still standing, it might no longer be tethered to the past. I imagined a paved driveway, a satellite dish, black electric lines looping through spruce trees.

Just as before, we turned south off the highway, felt the pavement give way to gravel, saw the power lines quit. But north of the two-track lane we were assaulted by a cluster of irate signs. END OF TOWN ROAD shouted the first, then, NO OUTLET, DEAD END, PRIVATE ROAD, NO TRESPASSING. The gravel road continued, but we weren't supposed to. Whoever posted those signs was angrier than Kathryn's gun-toting clammer.

I worried that the southern tip of the peninsula had been sold. The new owner might have torn the cabin down, not interested in a dwelling without electricity or running water. I might only find a strip of raw earth, scraps of green and red lumber, broken glass, bulldozer tracks. That image would forever overlay my memory of sitting around the table on nail kegs, traipsing under spruce trees, wandering the coast with my father.

A plat map would tell who owned the property. We turned around and started toward Milbridge in search of the town office. I imagined an ancient building with sloping floors that creaked underfoot, the air thick with the aroma of damp plaster and moldy paper. What I had conjured in my imagination had been retired in 2013 in favor of a new structure in a new location. We parked in front of a simple gray clapboard building with gable roof. It housed both the public library and the town office.

The new town office was efficient and well-lit: no fusty tomes stacked on wooden shelves, spooky corridors, bleak shadowy offices. With the help of a records clerk, I learned that a large block of land on the southern tip of the peninsula had been sold, but not the cabin or surrounding property. I obtained contact information for the owner and later we spoke by telephone. She was the daughter of the man who rented the cabin to my father, whose bones lay near the ocean. It was her son who was burning brush during our visit in 2007. She said that her mother purchased the land in 1934, paying less than one dollar a foot for 500 feet of ocean frontage.

"Ignore those signs and go back," she said. The new owner posted them, but her family still had right of access.

Again, I drove north and east on Route 1, down the gravel road toward the tip of the peninsula. I passed the signs and parked in a clearing surrounded by spruce trees. Near the cabin was a sign that read, "Wildlife and Friends, Welcome." The cabin looked the same, still had green siding and red trim. Even the free-standing outhouse was there. I peeked in a window, saw the nail kegs, the bunk room, caught a whiff of musty lumber.

In *Walking*, Henry David Thoreau laments the concept of private property, extolls the virtues of "...walking over the surface of God's earth." He wandered everywhere in the woods near Concord. In an early version of his essay, delivered as a lecture to the Concord Lyceum in 1851, Thoreau said: "But possibly the day will come when...fences shall be multiplied...to confine men to the *public* road, and walking over the surface of God's earth shall be construed to mean trespassing..." For me, that day had arrived.

Perhaps the new owner posted those signs because he was upset by curious tourists or locals who roamed his land when he wasn't there. When I visited with my parents, we hiked around the peninsula almost every evening. We never asked who owned the land, and no one ever stopped us.

I left the cabin behind, brushed through moist evergreen saplings toward the ocean. Reindeer moss crunched under my feet, stirring up the aroma of damp soil and decaying

Andrew C. Miller
Deer Isle, ME

wood. When I reached the rocky shoreline I stopped, leaning against a spindly spruce tree. The shoreline was shrouded in fog. Somewhere offshore, a lobster boat muttered along; the gentle thrum-thrum-thrum of diesel accompanied by the barely audible strains of country western music. Where the rocks gave way to water, a narrow swath of kelp and rock-weed undulated with the waves. Gulls glided in circles over-head, their black-tipped wings rigid and steady, their bodies tremulous in the breeze. Too bad the tide was in. Otherwise I'd scramble over the boulders and down to the pools, search out a few sea stars, maybe an urchin or two.

***

Brenda E. McDermott
Searsport, ME

79th Maine Soldier Takes His Life

In a dream I see a boy
building a tree house
in a forest of white birches
and evergreens and chirping
birds. I don't recognize him
and yet, I know him well.
I speak to him softly:

return to the woods,
restore that treehouse,
be in the place of wild things that
do not burden their lives with grief;
spend time with the sparrows and
listen to their soothing songs;
then, fold your anguish like a shroud,
and thrust it deep into the sweet earth.

Elmae Passineau
Weston, WI

Two Faces of Mom

The daily mass was at 8 am
  and Mom was usually there
Dad was in charge at home for the time being
  and permitted us ice cream for breakfast

In the living room,
  Mom's small grotto,
  statues, flowers, vigil lights,
  was prominently displayed,
And this is where the evening ritual ensued—
  on our knees praying the rosary,
  rote and boring and something merely endured,
  we counted the beads until we were freed

This woman, strict and religious,
  with her permed red hair,
  critical dark eyes,
  patterned housedress and apron,
  long before women ventured out of their housewife roles,
  went out,
  found herself a job in a paint store,
  and bought herself a full-length mink coat

F. Anthony D'Alessandro
Celebration, FL

Life's Bookmarks: Music and Song

Remember a song your mom sang to you?
Mine was Italian…"Batti mannini"…clap hands.
Remember a song from music class or school band, or an
    unplanned solo?
Mine was…"Footloose."
Remember a church melody while squeezing my baby's
    hand before an anticipated jungle deployment?
Mine was…"Day Is Done."
Remember a serenading song playing when savoring the
    seventh heaven your first crush?
Mine was…"Love Me Tender."
Remember a prom night song?
Mine was…"Dock of the Bay."
Remember a college favorite?
Mine was…"Traveling Man."
Remember a song crooned night and day by a more
    seasoned sibling?
Naval hero, my big bro hummed it repeatedly.
Mine was…"Stardust."
Remember a song on a somber, gloomy, grief laden day?
Mine was…"Leader of the Pack."
Remember songs played on school's final June day?
Mine was…"Surfin' USA."
Remember a song on accomplishment days, victories,
    new job?
Mine was…"We Are the Champions."
Remember songs playing when you married your dream
    love?
Mine were…"Fly Me to the Moon," and
    "The Way You Look Tonight."
Remember songs played at your daughter's wedding?

Continued

F. Anthony D'Alessandro
Celebration, FL

Mine was..."Daddy's Little Girl."
Remember songs guiding you throughout life?
Mine was..."My Way."
Remember songs guaranteed to deliver moisture to
    shorelines of your eyes?
Mine was..."Momma."
Remember a Golden Anniversary song?
Mine was..."Because You Loved Me."
Remember mystical melodies that delivered us to specific
    moments of life?
Mine were..."Mondo Cane," and "Home for Christmas."
Yes, they are life's bookmarks delivered by music and
melodies that escort our memories back thru our history.

***

Steve Troyanovich
Florence, NJ

autumn nocturne
>   My dreams...
>   are woven nightly in your voice...
>
>   —Miklos Radnoti

sometimes i feel like a lost river
meandering towards the brink
of dream's last harbor...

surrounded by the landscape
of your eyes
sirenlike your touch
guides me to the shelter
of tomorrow's shore

Sylvia Little-Sweat
Wingate, NC

Ireland

Dublin's *Book of Kells*
draws transatlantic tourists
like wires—magnetized.

National studs graze
in County Kildare pastures—
whinny bygone praise.

Belfast bells pealing
through the Northern Ireland chill
to gild the morning.

Rain, like bitter tears,
streaks Belfast's mural faces—
etches pain again.

Derry's city walls
recall a wind-sighed reprise
to Strife's melodies.

Vermillion skies
cast in Clew Bay's mirrored light—
dark-lapped elegies.

Northern Ireland bogs—
Gaelic on garrulous tongues,
sheep bleating echoes.

Helen Ackermann
Rothschild, WI

Nature Heals

Each morning is the same. I put out the bird feeder; one I can remove at night because of visiting bear threats. After all, he has been there once and destroyed the suet feeder. The birds come immediately. It is as if they are waiting for me to appear. I try to have their breakfast ready by 6:30 a.m. It is spring; after all, the light comes earlier. They come in a particular order. Usually the mourning doves arrive first, then blue jays, cardinals, white throated sparrows, red-wing blackbirds, grosbeaks, a variety of woodpeckers and of course the chickadees. Others, such as juncos may stop by as they travel through.

I can watch from my favorite spot in the sunroom as I spend time in prayer and meditation. Time has taken on a strange dimension during this time of the pandemic. Life has been turned upside down. During this writing in May, 2020, we have been asked, in Wisconsin, to stay sheltered at home. I miss the physical contact with others; children, grandchildren and friends. I am thankful for the companionship of a spouse.

We are all uprooted in a different way. We all want to return to normal knowing deep in our hearts that life will not be as we have known it before. We will grow into a new normal. I suppose this is why I need the rhythm of the birds. I need their coming and going to the bird feeder because I can count on them. There is little I can count on each day as the facts will change. There are more cases of Covid-19, more deaths and more pain and suffering. There is little pleasure I can count on in the midst of hearing all the depressing news. The birds fill the vacuum. They help me think more positively. As a result I can more fully appreciate the goodness of humanity.

Helen Ackermann
Rothschild, WI

I need the stability of the birds, which come each day
with regularity, giving me a sense of balance to begin my day.
Nature heals and gives a new promise of life.

***

Jeanine Stevens
Sacramento, CA

Nevada, Late Autumn

Lake shore, Canada geese
resilient to freezing
bob like toys in a carnival gallery.

We weave string
around the tender vine maple
protecting coming drifts.

Aspen leaves catch in skim ice,
curl and glitter
in a slower stream.

Soft sift of first snow,
nip and neigh,
wild horses in the next canyon,

living things following scrub grass,
needing to move on
to southern deserts.

Kristina Branch
Boothbay Harbor, ME

Bottle Green

It was 9 a.m. and there was an insistent knocking at the door. Her stomach did a flip-flop. *Oh my*, she thought, i*t can't be him*, but already she could hear his voice, his braying laugh. She knew the knocking would go on until his knuckles broke.

Lloyd showed up whenever he had something he could brag about. Something he could taunt her with. A new wife, an expensive car, a big promotion. This time it was all three. She wished she'd had some warning. She hadn't even combed her hair, but Lloyd's young bride looked fresh off the assembly line just like the sportscar in the driveway.

"Hey, can you believe I caught this babe?" Lloyd said. "You think she wants me for my money?" He pretended he was thumbing through dollar bills. "You should see my bank account! I'm a partner now—they begged me."

I can handle this, she thought, but then Lloyd dug in. He marched around the dining room, rolling his eyes.

"What the hell's this color?" he demanded. "Was it a discount buy?"

She shook her head. "It's only the first coat," she said. "It's not finished yet."

"Oh, give me a break!" Lloyd shouted. "It looks like slime!"

"Excuse me," she said evenly, "but since you didn't call ahead, I'm going upstairs to fix my face."

As she left the room, she heard Lloyd saying, "Fix her face? Is she kidding? If she could fix it, I wouldn't have dumped her."

Buttoning her bathrobe, she left by the back door and went into the shed behind the house. The paint was one more thing that Lloyd had ruined for her, and she knew she'd never look at it again without thinking of the things he'd said. She was glad she'd only used one can. Perhaps the

Kristina Branch
Boothbay Harbor, ME

hardware store would take the other back.

Lloyd had never liked the things she liked, the things she chose. He mocked and needled her relentlessly throughout their life together, but because she cared for him, she convinced herself that he wasn't really cruel, he just liked to tease. But in the dim light of the shed, she felt a burning deep inside her rise up to her throat. *She* had left the marriage, and this morning, in her kitchen, Lloyd had taken her one defiant act and claimed it for himself.

She pried the lid off the remaining can of *Bottle Green*. Stirring slowly with a paint stick, she watched the pigments swirl into a forest mass of vines and leaves and then a mossy shore. It was beautiful. How sad for Lloyd to hate it. But despite it all, she felt that he deserved a second chance. She picked up the can and walked outside. Perhaps he'd like the color better when he saw it poured all over his new Porsche.

***

E. H. Gerard
Penobscot, ME

A Regular Spider, I Am

No strings, we said.
Yet, unconsciously I spun
A thread for love
A thread for commitment.

No Strings, of course,
And I laughed.
Until, I tried to walk away
And couldn't—Snagged
In my own web.

the late Jim Harnedy
Machiasport, ME

A Mystic Bloom

In January 1977, Jane and I celebrated our anniversary in the Dominican Republic. It was our first trip to the Caribbean, and we were in awe of the beauty of the island, but its political appearance, infrastructure and poverty depicted it as a third world country.

In spite of the negative issues we encountered, the natural beauty inspired us to want to return to the Caribbean. Thankfully, over the next three decades, we were able to spend many wonderful vacations in these tropical paradise islands.

One of the standout beauties we found growing wild everywhere were multi-colored hibiscus. At one place where we stayed in St. Thomas, the maid would replace a fresh vase of hibiscus flowers each day. Jane and I hoped that someday we could acquire a plant, but first we would have to learn how to care for one.

In 1979, we purchased our home in Maine. It was an old cape in the town of Boothbay. Concurrent with our purchase, Jane was launching herself on a new career as a painter. She had left her position as an administrative manager of a large mental health clinic in Massachusetts to study art. Shortly after we moved to Boothbay she became friends with a professional artist, Norman Andrews. Norm did water colored landscapes and seascapes, as well as pastel portraits.

In the early fall of 1979, Jane and Norm trekked up to the Camden area to enjoy a plein air day, capturing the autumn sea. Upon completing their painting, they spotted a lovely nursery and decided to see what was inside the greenhouses. This adventure yielded that there were a number of hibiscus plants. When Norm learned of how we loved hibiscus and hoped to someday have one, he gifted Jane with our first

the late Jim Harnedy
Machiasport, ME

plant that very day.

Over the next two years, we converted our old cape Boothbay home into a modern, environmentally designed home with two solar panel greenhouses, and our early collection of hibiscus plants. After moving to Bucks Harbor, Machiasport, in 1998, our plant population had to adjust to a non-solar greenhouse environment. The hibiscus continued to grow but flowering became a problem. Our only hibiscus with yellow flowers last bloomed in 2012.

On December 14, 2017, Jane passed away after battling breast cancer for 27 years. This event set the stage for a mystical surprise. On January 30, 2018, what would have been Jane's 84th birthday, a beautiful yellow hibiscus flower bloomed.

The mysticism has continued with a large pink flowering hibiscus blooming on my birthday, October 15, 2019. During that time, our daughter, Sandi, was visiting from South Carolina, and a second bloom made its appearance to wish Sandi a Happy Birthday on October 25th.

Two months later on December 14, 2019, the second anniversary of my wife, Jane's passing, the mystical yellow hibiscus burst forth once again, reminding me that our loved ones are always with us.

Liz Mockler
Randolph, ME

Dream Home

I live in a little house
near a little pond
wrapped by
towering twisted
trees that seem
to touch the heavens
and protect me
from the world
even in winter
when their bare
wrinkled limbs
strike against
each other
like swords
to the death
and the wind
hums its sad
mourning cry
and for a moment
there are only
the lonesome sighs
to mark the end
of another day
in a little house
near a little pond

Lucia Owen
Stoneham, ME

Intersection

When you were in the Veterans' Home and
had learned at last to get in and out of the car
we took off to explore all the back roads
we could think of.
We knew them all, each hill,
after a lifetime up here but I had to get you out.
You so hated going back.

Once, after missing where we should have turned
to find the place we thought we were going
and the road turned to dirt then to tar again,
we came to an intersection
we simply didn't recognize.
How could that be?
We drove through then got silly with surprise.
Who knew this was that road
at the top of the hill in Mechanic Falls?
We hadn't been lost,
just turned around.

When you finally came home,
barely half-healed,
we never doubted
that the familiar moves—
how to get out of bed, get dressed,
talk to each other,
how to live in this house—
would all be waiting just as we left them
until those first nights and they weren't.

Lucia Owen
Stoneham, ME

Now each day they morph into alien uphills
we cannot scale.
We have no map
for this new landscape,
so turned around
from where we used to be,
no new route to get us up the Eiger
we tried to climb the day before
and we have no idea
where we are, still together
at this next intersection
in our lives.

***

Sister Irene Zimmerman
Greenfield, WI

Encounter

I met a fawn today,
or I could say
a fawn met me.

We both stood
as still as we could
and looked at each other
with curious eye
across the divide
(barely fifteen feet wide)
of our creaturehood,

then with white-tipped tail
it waved goodbye
and moved leisurely into the wood.

Deborah LeFalle
San Jose, CA

That Annoying Beep

the one that...
    awakens you
    in the middle of the night

    startles you every few minutes
    despite your attempts to ignore it

you...
    put your head under your pillow
    in hopes of muffling the sound

    try to subconsciously will it away
    but find you are no match

    wanna throw a shoe at it
    but fear you'll break something

    finally relent and decide
    to answer its desperate plea

knowing...
    by giving *it* new life
    you may just save yours.

Sally Taylor
Sedgwick, ME

What Sonny Saw

"Mama. It's screaming, Mama." Sonny charged through the screen door, chubby legs pumping, arms outstretched, and he halted at his mother's chair, where muddy water seeped around his feet onto the old pine floor.

"Oh, Sonny, again? Your shorts are wet. That's way too deep. You don't have your life jacket on...." His mother, Jazz, turned to consider him with a slight frown. Her reading glasses glinted in the sunlight bouncing off the lake.

"N-no," Sonny, deflected from his excitement, paused to examine his toes, black with mud. "I... I just looking...."

"Sonny, you know the rules. When you're down there by yourself...."

"Daddy's fishing." Sonny's voice lilted hopefully.

"Hmm." Despite her show, Jazz wasn't as angry as she might have been. She knew her boy to be cautious, and if Conner was fishing from the dock, she would be mollified. "So, Daddy's on the dock, or... in the boat?" He might, she guessed, be drifting off in pursuit of some elusive fish.

Sonny hesitated. His father probably warned him to stay away from the water before paddling away. But Sonny hadn't paid much attention. Now, his four-year old brain struggled, finally deciding for truth, afraid his mother would check his story.

"Canoe. The canoe," Sonny offered, making a paddling motion.

"Ah," Jazz nodded, compressing her lips. She saw clearly enough into both son and husband. And she judged—half annoyed, half resigned—that Conner, in the canoe, was by now far across the lake, fully absorbed in dangling his lure over the side. Assuredly he had not met their agreed upon conditions for properly supervising Sonny. He had to be close by for Sonny to be allowed in the water without a life jacket,

Sally Taylor
Sedgwick, ME

even though he could swim, even though it was shallow. She sighed. She figured Sonny, young as he was, understood the key points. But Conner? She shut her eyes in brief frustration.

Except Jazz had no desire to make a fuss on this lovely morning, while she might yet steal the chance to read, uninterrupted, for another hour. She shifted in her seat, gazing into Sonny's hopeful face, turned up, not quite level with hers. Such sweet long lashes, and those rounded cheeks recalled pictures of herself as a child.

Jazz saw his mouth relaxing and registered almost before she knew it herself that he saw she was weakening and unlikely to act upon his infraction. He might not understand completely but he could sense that the comfort—warm sunshine, pillows in the deep wicker chair, a book on her lap, hot coffee at her right hand—all conspired in his favor. *You clever little fellow*, she smiled inwardly, *you know*. His mouth by now curved into an impish smile. She tousled his brown curls, several locks bleached almost red by the sun.

"Okay, Sonny, okay. I know you are careful. Remember, Mama counts on you to be very, very careful." And she deepened her tone to invest it with solemnity. Sonny met her eyes and nodded. Her seriousness registered. Getting off this time was an exception, one of many perhaps, but an exception, nonetheless.

Sufficiently content, Jazz turned back to her reading, only Sonny's grimy hand pulled hard at the hem of her shirt.

"Bu...but Mama." Sonny's voice turned breathless, impatient. "It's a bird, a big bird." His arms flung wide to show how big. "And a snake. They're wrestling, Mama, the snake and the bird."

"Really?" Jazz blinked, distracted again from her novel. While she gloried that Sonny, young as he was, observed the world with enthusiasm, still the book tugged her away from him, from the entire scene. Her own summer indulgence, a detective story—the female sleuth about to slip into bed with an excessively handsome colleague, this very minute realizing he was her major suspect.

"The bird with the white head! The big bird, with the white head! They go over and over. Water splashing, woof!" Sonny, excited again, swayed his naked torso back and forth, flopping his arms downward several times, as though slapping the surface of the water.

"Was it the eagle, then?" Jazz was skeptical.

"Maybe, the eagle," Sonny said, made cautious by her doubts.

"And a snake? Certainly a fish...."

"Not fish, Mama... no, no, snake... it's screaming...."

"A screaming snake?" And Jazz's eyes went wide. Sonny nodded emphatically. Well, he had got her now, Jazz thought, rising quickly from her chair. "Let's go see. Do you suppose they're still there?" She grabbed his hand, heading for the door to the deck.

At the end of the short dock—motoring skiff moored and canoe indeed gone—Sonny jumped up and down eagerly, pointing toward the east side of the lake.

"There, Mama, there. See?"

Jazz could see violent turmoil in the arm of the lake between them and a small promontory, spikey with fir trees, shore edged with lichened boulders. She wished she had thought to grab the binoculars. The area was dappled in sun and shadow, making it difficult to sort out what was happening.

"There, they were there, before," said Sonny, pointing further left, nearer to the swimming float they shared with the neighboring cottage, occupied this year by strangers. Jazz had observed them attempting to sunbathe on the pebbly shore. She shivered with distaste at this flaw in the placidity of her summer, this disruption to her escape from work—her own and Conner's—that she craved almost the entire winter.

"See, see, Mama? The snake—he got it. He got it. He

Sally Taylor
Sedgwick, ME

shakes, back and forth." And he swung body and arms yet more wildly. Jazz jerked her mind back from her unpleasant neighbor to focus on the huge bird and its twisting prey.

"Sonny, you're so right. It is the eagle. See the size of his wings! They're gigantic. And his white tail, all splayed out like that." She paused, trying to make sense of the confusing struggle in the uneven light. "Gracious, that's not a snake. It's another bird. Oh my gosh, the eagle is on the other bird's back! With his talons, he's pressing it under the water." Her voice had dropped to a whisper.

"But what's that, Mama? What's that long thing? He's shaking it. See?" Sonny's voice too was hushed. With his hand in his mother's, he felt her stiffening.

"It's a duck, Sonny. No, no, it's too big. It's a cormorant. That's its neck. He's killing the cormorant. That's why you heard the scream. Before. It was the cormorant." The cormorant protesting its terror and pain, she thought, shuddering.

"Why're you whispering, Mama?" Sonny asked. Jazz looked down at him, achingly fond, her eyes full with tears.

She didn't know how to answer, so as to be faithful, and so he would understand, but in a way that would still leave whole and entire his sense of this place, of the summer, of the world they lived in, as fundamentally good and safe.

"They're magnificent," she said more normally, pulling back from her desire to cry. "Magnificent, both of them. Strong, determined....completely awesome."

"'termined, Mama?"

"They don't give up. God made them. And they won't give up." Her voice trembled though she meant to be firm. She felt unprepared. A vastness in the universe she had not glimpsed before now showed so starkly.

"It's dead, Mama. See? See? The black one's dead."

"You're right, Sonny. Now the eagle has food for his children...I guess."

"He will eat," Sonny said, matter-of-factly. "He eats so he

gets strong." The wild thrashing had stopped. Nothing now, except the waves from the eagle's wings as he swam, heaving himself steadily toward shore, cormorant clasped tight underneath. Sonny dropped his mama's hand and started to turn back to the pebbly mud where he had been interrupted in his explorations.

"Where's Dad?" he asked, for suddenly his mama seemed unaccountably far away. He understood the excitement was finished. But Mama was standing, rigid, remote, her hand shading her eyes from the sun, gazing across the glittering lake southward to the far end.

"He took the canoe?" she asked in a funny voice.

"For fishing, Mama." Sonny sounded a small note of scorn.

"Was someone with him?" Jazz dropped her voice again, soft and pinched. "There's two people in that canoe."

"That lady," Sonny answered waving toward the neighboring cottage, his childish voice unconcerned. "Daddy said she wants fish. Tonight, can we eat fish?"

Jazz nodded mechanically, still watching what she hoped Sonny could not see in the distance.

Two profiles, dark against the sparkling wavelets, reaching toward each other, cautiously so as not to tip the canoe— turned to a single scar on her retina. Her hand fell, body shuddering, lips tight to shut off the scream. And her heart wretched with sympathy for the cormorant, still pinned under the heaving, clawing eagle, strangled by the vicious tearing beak.

Denise Pendleton
Belfast, ME

Red Leaf

I.
The first red leaf
of autumn stills your heart
as you climb the porch steps
dripping the lake wet happiness
of an August swim. You don't want to see
what signals the inevitable end to barefoot,
bare-skinned days so few and fleeting
in this northernmost state that is home.

II.
Regret hasn't yet set in of all you didn't give them
this summer of their childhood, when this
is the time, the time a drumbeat for making
memories in a vacationland where joy
is so briefly close at hand, as in the cold
cascading waves you finally dare
to wade into and ride to keep up with one child,
urge the other forward, before the wave slips
away into what is only a matter of time.

III.
September harvest moon—the brightest
of the year. Who can sleep when it shines,
polished by the exuberance of summer
still spilling forth its bounty of cucumbers, corn,
tomatoes, and apples with their warm juice
a surprise when picked off the branch—oh why
do the crickets wait until now to sing
and sing their ceaseless asking, an insistence
you cannot close your windows on.

Denise Pendleton
Belfast, ME

IV.
How the light changes, softens into hues.
The clouds mingle their dark and light, their movement
brings your eyes to them to feast
on their changing forms. What has been
sleeping within, what part of you
have you forgotten? Who is it that appears now
startled by the sweetness of this invitation,
as from an old friend you'd forgotten who brings
a map for turning inward, helps you dig
happily for wool sweaters, find slippers
for cold floors, and be glad for the complication
of color that floods the hills and flares along roadsides.

V.
As you begin your journey, the words come and you sing
your way toward the diminishment of even this
loveliness stripped away then teasing the eye
to find pleasure in how a tree's branches now bare
release beauty to the winter sky
marked more by darkness than light.

Gerry Di Gesu
Union, NJ

Spring Day

Dangling prisms refract comets of color and hope
across stark walls of my kitchen and heart

The cat stalks a rabbit which becomes
a frozen statue hidden behind red tulips

Squirrels and jays battle at the feeder

The phone
death of a friend, prayers for my daughter,
my husband's soft voice

Mail
hope for a cancer patient, birth of a baby

I write letters, essays, poems

Late rays of sun slant through the window
and form a golden orb of promise
enveloping daffodils in a green bowl

Light rests on forsythia reaching for joy
from a vase in a corner of the room

This beauty existed last spring but was unseen

Today I taste peace

Kitty Hartford
Boothbay Harbor, ME

The Dump

My daughter Michelle saved all the newspaper clippings, flyers, posters, and councilmen's reports, which she incorporated into her 7th grade social studies project. She even included the four-foot high Stinkometer that we'd hung on the kitchen wall next to the big window that faced the back yard.

Rockland was notorious for its smell. Most of the sardine-packing canneries had closed, but the putrid fish waste still bubbled beneath the thin layer of dirt spread periodically over the trash in the landfill—an old limestone quarry. "Camden by the Sea, and Rockland by the Smell."

We lived just an alder patch away from the city dump. When we bought the house in 1974, we couldn't see or smell the dump. We knew it was nearby, but it wasn't until a few seasons later that it became a problem. Marine Colloids' slop, the byproduct left from processing seaweed into carrageenan, was the biggest contributor to the odor.

The laundry came in off the clothesline smelling like smoky fermenting garbage. Backyard cookouts had to be planned around not just fair weather, but fair winds. On hot summer nights, the kids were often awakened by a rancid breeze coming into their bedrooms. "Mom! I can't sleep! It stinks in here!" They were literally gagging.

This was unacceptable! Our rights to the peaceful enjoyment of our own little private paradise were being threatened. We couldn't do anything outdoors...no badminton, no running through the sprinkler, no climbing the maple trees. The kids pedaled their bikes as fast as they could, away from the dump. Still, their hair reeked, their clothes stank, their eyes stung.

What to do? All the neighbors had been complaining for years. Time to take drastic action—take it to the streets. Take

Kitty Hartford
Boothbay Harbor, ME

it to the town officials.

And, so we did. Meetings started at my house but soon became too big for my living room. The flyers we stapled to the phone poles invited people to attend the city council meetings. Petitions were signed, the subject was on the agenda at the city council meetings, month after month, tabled, tweaked, appealed.

The dump smell was front-page news in the *Courier-Gazette* and appeared in the "Elsewhere" section of the *Portland Press Herald*. People were talking, loudly. And we were heard. With the Stink-a-Meter in tow, along with a few experts to add some weight to our testimonies, we faced city hall, and we won!

Eight years later, that little house sold quickly and a new subdivision was carved out of the alder patch. The dump is still there, but the smell lingers no longer.

***

Sylvia Little-Sweat
Wingate, NC

In Memoriam
To Keith Cannon and Others

Morning breaks colder than before.
Oak leaves curl in winter's wake.
Red suns hemorrhage against the sky.
Tundra chill steels the day. Near dusk
A black swirl of starlings circles down,
Lands in bare trees, shrills its mutiny.
Ice anneals all fallow fields. Even
Time seems to thaw, to disappear like
Yesterday's snow, the tracks of deer.

Tom Fallon
Rumford, ME

Katahdin

It was solid
the mountain
as painted on the canvas,
it was clearly made of rock,
Marsden Hartley returning home
to live
in Maine
after years of traveling in abstraction,
the mountain in Maine solid
rising into the sky
rock,
and the Maine native painted the mountain true,
it was a creation, with white pine
Mount Katahdin
rising from the earth, forested
cold white with first snow.

***

Steve Troyanovich
Florence, NJ

...the homeless dawn

No smoldering in their aloneness
memories mourn yesterday
maverick winds and bursting sunset
burn against tomorrow's sky...
somewhere tears must dream of other voices

Sherry Ballou Hanson
Portland, OR

Wind

I am wind and earth is my command.
I sneak among grasses all silky and whispery
dart at critters, lift up the eagle,
tear into tree tops tossing branches
rock a single leaf in a fiery maple.
I am divine.

I scud across the marsh,
murmur among reeds, tickle the legs
of graceful blue heron, scare up
green-headed mallards and dive
at a shoal of herring.
I am elemental.

On wild traces of southern seas
I howl in troughs, boost albatross,
rip into a pyramid of sail
rattling rigging, snicking the shrouds.
I've brought many a wreck
To vast and pitiless wastes
where man chases silver fish
on blue water. I am relentless.

On the trades I carry pollen and fragrance
move clouds, eddy down a moonbeam,
bring the diaphanous dusk and balance
sheets and sheets of rain.
At the vortex I am ruin.

I am steady at the poles
star fire, sun fire,
I am forever.

Carolyn S. Nevin
Nashua, NH

The Crossroads

12:15 PM
It's not like Angie to be late. I'll just keep waiting.
I picked up the mystery I kept in my car for times like these. I was almost finished with one Angie had lent me called *B is for Burglar*. So far it was better that its predecessor, *A is for Alibi*. *Maybe Angie got involved in a conversation with her mom. Read your book, Carolyn!*

12:30 PM
We did agree to meet at noon, right?
The book's main character was a thirty-something female private investigator named Kinsey Millhone, a strong and brave woman. She reminded me of Angie. I plopped the book face down onto the passenger seat and looked around for my missing friend. *How about M is for Missing when the author gets there in the alphabet?*
Traffic was light on Route 119, the secondary road between the small cities of Alabaster and Montevallo. Three pick-up trucks sped by before I ever spotted a car. It wasn't Angie's. Besides, she would be coming out to Route 119 where Route 22 crossed the road.
Angie's plan was to go home, change clothes, and make sure her mom would be home for the kids when they got off the school bus. I would do the same. After that we would meet here at Moore's Crossroads, where she would leave her car, and I would drive us to lunch.
My house was only two streets beyond the crossroads toward Montevallo, but Angie's was way out in Columbiana, a distance of maybe twenty-five miles round trip. From the snack bar at the university it was a good thirty minutes to her house, then another twenty back here to the crossroads. Maybe there was some traffic on the county roads between

Carolyn S. Nevin
Nashua, NH

here and there. If Angie was unlucky enough to get behind a pulp-wood truck filled with felled pines trees, that would explain the delay.

Angie and I were both looking forward to a celebratory lunch and an afternoon of conversation. It was Friday, the last day of the semester. We had coffee together in the snack bar a few hours earlier to decompress.

"What was your last final?" Angie asked. "Mine was Ed Psyche, and it was easy."

"Mine was that boring testing and measurement class. Actually, all I had to do this morning was to turn in a paper. The final was Tuesday night, the same time the class met every week. It was rough taking that class the same semester as my practice teaching at the high school. I had no choice. I need to graduate next week and start looking for a teaching job in January."

"Lucky you," Angie said. "I still have three semesters left. And now I am having second thoughts about teaching."

"Really?"

"Yep. Since the divorce, I have been stressed about money," Angie said. "Even with child support from Jack, which isn't much, teaching won't pay enough."

"That's for sure," I agreed. "Especially if you plan to teach here in Alabama. What would you do instead?"

"I could go back to nursing school and finish in maybe a year. And I could make a lot more money as a nurse than as a teacher."

"Wait a minute! I thought you didn't like nursing school." I was surprised at the change in Angie's thinking.

"Well, now that I am the main breadwinner, I have to be smarter about things," Angie said.

"That makes sense. I couldn't have considered teaching if it weren't going to be our second income. Hey, what are you doing the rest of the day?" I asked.

"Nothing planned, really. Why?"

"Let's go to lunch somewhere decent. Then we can take

our time and talk about our plans. We both may be starting new lives in '87!"

"Sounds great! I'll have to go back to the house first and ask Mom to take care of the kids after school," Angie said. "It shouldn't be a problem."

"Me, too. I have to get out of these sweats and make sure my mom will be home when Daniel gets off the bus," I said.

"Okay!" Angie was getting excited about the idea. "Where should we go for lunch?"

"How about some place on the way to Birmingham?" I asked. "Even Shoney's would seem like luxury right about now. We'll have lots of choices if we head up Highway 31 toward Pelham."

"Okay. Who's driving?"

"Let me!" I offered. "Since you have to drive out to the sticks and back, why don't we meet at Moore's Crossroads? You can leave your car there, and I'll drive the rest of the way."

"Sounds like a plan," Angie said. I think I can make it back to the crossroads by noon. How's that?"

"Great!" I said. "It's time we had some fun! Let's go."

We got up from the table, left the snack bar, and headed for our respective vehicles.

12:45 PM
I am waiting until 1 PM. If she is not here by then, I am going home to call her.

In B is for Burglar, Kinsey was about to enter an empty house, at night, in the dark, to look for a potentially dangerous criminal. I was having difficulty concentrating on her problems. I was dealing with a mystery of my own.

1:15 PM
I was home. I called Angie's house, but there was no answer. There was no answer at her mother's house, either. Her mom's house was right next door. Theirs were the only

Carolyn S. Nevin
Nashua, NH

two houses out there in a desolate-looking new subdivision just outside downtown Columbiana. Angie's parents had built their home first. Then Angie, Jack, and their three kids lived in a double wide trailer on their lot while their own home was being built. The construction took nearly two years, and the family of five was ecstatic when they finally moved in. Angie invited me to the house-warming party about this time last year.

But then the marriage broke apart. Jack moved out and Angie and the kids stayed in the house. The best thing was that Angie had her mother right next door to help with the kids while she attended classes to earn a teaching degree.

3:30 PM
Daniel was home from school watching TV with a neighbor friend. Mom volunteered to fix dinner for us that night. Tom would not be home until nearly 6 PM.

After calling both Angie and her mom multiple times, I decided to head for Columbiana.

I drove the short mile to Moore's Crossroads and took a right onto Highway 22. Like all our county roads, it was two-laned. The brightest color in my field of view was the double yellow line warning drivers not to pass. More than once while I traveled this road, a vehicle would defy the law and pass another car on this stretch, which contained four dips. When you were down in a dip, so to speak, you were invisible to oncoming cars until you got to the top of the dip. Then the road plunged you into the next dip. I watched as far ahead as possible, relieved to see no oncoming traffic. When I saw Shelby Academy, a small private school coming up on the right, I knew I had safely navigated that series of unnerving dips.

The rest of the drive was visually boring. The day was dreary, but no rain was expected. The roadside was populated with the remains of dried up weeds, and the only color aside from the lines on the road was from the scattered

Carolyn S. Nevin
Nashua, NH

stands of southern pines so ubiquitous in Alabama. Just a few miles from the turn-off to Angie's subdivision, I was slowed by a pulp-wood truck creeping snail-like uphill. I became anxious and a bit jumpy. Angie was almost four hours late meeting me. I scanned the roadside for signs of trouble, unsure of what I was looking for. There had been no signs of traffic or highway construction. Something wasn't right.

I pulled into Angie's driveway. Her car was missing. I rang the doorbell, hoping to see her younger son race to let me in. No answer. I walked across Angie's front yard and across her mom's front yard and up to the door. I rang the bell. No answer. No vehicles in the driveway. Complete quiet all around me. Dead stalks of goldenrod and scrub grasses stood silently waving in a meager breeze, watching me make my way slowly back to my car, head hung low.

That evening was difficult. I made it through dinner and watched a little TV with my husband. But I could not stop thinking about Angie. I tried reading my book but couldn't focus. I had my own mystery to solve. By the time I went to bed around 11 PM, I had called both Angie's house and her mom's several times. There was still no answer.

The next day was not much better. I busied myself organizing the messy piles of papers and books that had been accumulating all semester in the corner of our bedroom I laughingly called my office. I asked Tom to help me bring the Christmas decorations up from the basement, and I made a valiant attempt to get interested in the task of making our home merry for the holidays. But my heart wasn't in it. Daniel had been invited to the movies with some friends, and Mom was back in her TV room writing notes for Christmas cards. I asked Tom to drive out to Columbiana with me to look for signs of Angie and her family.

The trip was a repeat of the previous day. No vehicles were in either driveway. No one answered either door. I didn't know what to do next. Tom wanted to help, but he had no

Carolyn S. Nevin
Nashua, NH

answers either. In my head I could hear Mom say, "No news is good news."

I could think of no way to stop worrying.

Sunday, 11 AM
On the second ring, I grabbed the phone.
"Hello?" I said.
"Who's this?" A young-sounding female voice asked.
"Who's THIS?" I practically shouted.
"It's Jenny. Mom's been writing this number on the sheets, and I needed to call and see whose it was."
"Jenny? Angie's Jenny?" I asked.
"Yes, it's me." She sounded shaky.
"This is your mom's friend, Carolyn." I said. "Where are you? Where's your mom? What in the world happened?" The questions kept tumbling out.
"Mom was in a wreck. She's in the hospital." Jenny's voice broke into sobs. "She's hurt really bad. And she can't even talk. They wired her jaw shut."
"Oh Sweetie!" My heart was breaking for the little girl who was about to turn twelve in a month. She must be terrified.
"Take some deep breaths. Then tell me what you can," I said.

Over the next thirty minutes, Jenny told me a chilling tale. Angie was travelling on Highway 22 toward Moore's Crossroads just past Shelby Academy. A pick-up truck coming from the opposite direction passed on the solid yellow line and hit Angie's car head-on. The impact drove the steering wheel into Angie's lower face and throat, crushing he jaw and damaging her windpipe.

She was air-lifted by helicopter to Caraway Medical Center in Birmingham where she still remained in ICU. Jenny said her mom kept moving her right hand in the air. Finally, her son guessed that Angie wanted something to write with. After one of the nurses supplied a pen, Angie wrote a phone number on the sheet beside her right thigh.

Carolyn S. Nevin
Nashua, NH

By the third writing of the same number, the family realized Angie wanted them to call the number. That was when Jenny went to the nurses' station to use the phone.

Jenny's story left me shaken, but somewhat relieved. Before we hung up, she promised to let me know as soon as I could visit her mom in the hospital. She promised to give Angie a gentle hug for me and tell her I was here for her if she or the kids needed anything.

After I hung up, my own family was anxious to hear the details. I tried to reconstruct the timeline of events. Angie had to have been close to the crossroads when she was hit. It must have happened on that one mile stretch of dangerous dips. The accident may even have happened while I waited in my car at the crossroads. Or it could have happened even before I arrived—according to my watch—at 11:59. I remembered being glad that I wasn't late for our meeting.

Months later Angie explained how she signaled the paramedics that she could barely breathe and was choking on her own blood. Her unfinished nursing training came in handy. It was her ability to remain calm that cued them to call for the helicopter. The rapid response by everyone involved helped save her life.

Later I learned that the driver of the pick-up truck was a sixteen-year-old student in one of my biology classes during my practice teaching experience. She had just gotten her driver's license. She got off with a broken ankle. Had she learned her lesson about passing on a double solid line? One could hope.

Two weeks after Jenny's Sunday morning call, I went to visit Angie. Jenny brought her out of her hospital room in a wheelchair, explaining that Angie was anxious to get up and moving as soon as possible. I barely recognized my friend. Her lower jaw was crisscrossed with stitches. She could not talk, and I could tell there was no way she could open her mouth to eat solid food yet.

Jenny was wonderful. She spoke for her mom, giving an

Carolyn S. Nevin
Nashua, NH

update on her condition. Angie would need extensive reconstructive dental work for sure.

I did not stay long that first day. Even the ten minutes I spent there was a strain for all of us, mostly Angie, who so badly wanted to talk. On the verge of tears, I leaned over and kissed Angie on the forehead. As I drew away, a tear did escape from the corner of my eye. I gave Jenny a hug, told her to call me if she needed anything, and left.

It took more than a year for Angie to recover from her injuries. Early in 1987, she moved herself and her three children into an apartment in Birmingham. She needed to be closer to her doctors and dentists. She sold the house in Columbiana.

Over Easter weekend that same year, my husband, Tom, took a job in a medium-sized city a hundred miles to the northeast. Daniel, my mom, and I stayed in our house in Montevallo until Daniel finished school in May. We finally found a house in Gadsden and moved there in the summer of 1987 in time for Daniel to start the sixth grade at a new school and for me to begin my first official teaching job at the tender age of forty. Over the next twenty-five years I taught high school science. By the time I retired, I discovered I most loved teaching chemistry, a class I had hated in high school.

Meanwhile, Angie took a giant step toward reinventing herself by joining the US Army. Since she was still under thirty-five years old when she signed up, the Army would pay for her nursing training. She had solved her financial difficulties.

We exchanged cards and letters for the next several years. In the one photo I have of her she is dressed in full combat gear grinning broadly from under her helmet with her reconstructed smile. You would never guess that she had nearly been killed just a few years earlier. In the note she included with her picture, she bragged about being combat qualified with a rifle—not so much bragging in the description of having to run a mile in full battle gear.

Carolyn S. Nevin
Nashua, NH

Shortly after I received the note and picture, she was shipped off to Kosovo as part of a peace keeping force. She wrote about dealing with three inches of mud in her tent, but she also wrote about how much fun she had going skiing in Austria. Back in the States, she was stationed in Colorado, and she and the kids went mountain climbing on several occasions.

In the Christmas card I received from her in 1997, Angie reported that the boys were still with her, but Jenny had gone back to Alabama to live with her dad and attend Jefferson State Community College. After that we lost touch.

We were never able to meet at Moore's Crossroads that Friday back in December of 1986. But we had become friends when each of us was at a crossroads in our lives. Some would describe what we were going through as a mid-life crisis. However, I prefer to think of our experiences being non-traditional students as training for reinventing ourselves.

After more than twenty years living our respective reinvented lives, I have some questions for Angie. Where do you live now? Did you remarry? How are the children? Are there grandchildren? Do you have an iPhone or an android? Wouldn't cell phones have come in handy back in 1986 when you went missing from Moore's Crossroads? Did you all survive the pandemic of 2020? And hey, did you read the rest of those Sue Grafton's alphabet mysteries we started reading together? If so, were you as sad as I was when Sue Grafton passed away before she had Kinsey turn forty in *Z is for Zero?*

It's time to get on social media and find Angie. Surely, she's out there somewhere. She should be easier to find now than she was that day she never showed up at the crossroads.

Ray Lani
Patchogue, NY

Maybe

(Chorus)
Maybe
We could stop fighting long enough
To find a cure for us all
Left or right black or white
Large or small short or tall
Maybe maybe

It's a crazy world
Birds are flying north
Yes it's all gone wrong
Maybe life lives on
And the birds can sing
Will there be a song
We have Covid-19
The corona virus disease
Our divided country
Has a new enemy

(Chorus)

(solo over verse)

(Chorus)

These are crazy times
Where the world has stopped
And no sports are played
And no songs are sung
And no money's made
And we're all afraid

(continued)

Ray Lani
Patchogue, NY

We have Covid-19
The corona virus disease
Our divided country
Has a new enemy

(Chorus)

***

Elmae Passineau
Weston, WI

Root Beer, Anyone?

In those days, we just remembered—
   no numbers on windshields,
   no microphones to carry orders inside
We took the order at the car window
   and turned it in at the carhop window
On sultry summer evenings,
   the parking lot would fill
   with a couple dozen cars

One hot August night,
   I picked up a metal tray
   laden with mugs of frothy A&W root beer,
   warm hot dogs, and crispy chips,
   turned away from the window,
   faced the swarm of cars,
   and stopped dead
I had no idea which car
   had ordered this tray

Andrea Suarez Hill
Jonesboro, ME

August

The shore shows its bones,
worn shells and stones.

A storm brewing out to sea.
carries Atlantic winds east.

Beach pebbles yield little for pickers,
but their laughter overlays waves.

Rose hips grow like tomatoes
and ravens swoop over berries.

A speckled white gull treads beside me,
our steps in sync.

Tired of flight,
feathers in our wake,

we sit to brood
on seaweed-covered sand
and dreams.

Alvaro de Araujo
Garland, TX

The Last of Midnight

Midnight had been missing for three days. She had never been out for so long and we began to worry. First we thought she could have been run over by a car. But cats are pretty smart, and Midnight was one of the smartest. She always looked both ways before crossing the road. It was unlikely she had had an accident, unless some mean dog or an "uncatty" person had been chasing her.

We also thought about the two Dobermans that belonged to our next door neighbor whose property was surrounded by high walls. At night our cat enjoyed climbing up that wall to watch the dogs. She knew the Dobermans couldn't jump that high and also that the only time they ran loose on the grounds was after sundown. So, during the day Midnight would jump down from the wall, first making sure the dogs were locked up in their cage, and then walk around the property at will. They could see and sniff her, and they would bark and growl in frustration. I'm sure her boldness bothered them. Could those dogs be holding a grudge against her? Had she gotten careless maybe and been surprised by one of them?

Then we remembered that cats have nine lives so there was a chance she could still be alive. Or could she? Who knows how many of those lives Midnight had already wasted in her nightly walks?

On the night of the fourth day she showed up in our backyard. She must have dragged herself there because she could hardly walk. Dried blood and dirt covered her black fur. In agony she cried and her cries cut right through my heart. I lifted Midnight, holding her shaky body against my chest, and went into the house. As I set her down on her favorite cushion and proceeded to clean her face and body with a warm damp towel, she stopped crying. In a short time

Alvaro de Araujo
Garland, TX

the brilliance irradiating from her eyes started flickering like the flame of a candle caught in a draft. She uttered several short meows as if trying to communicate with me. I sensed she was saying goodbye. Now it was my turn to weep.

She stopped breathing. I looked into her eyes for the last time and, seconds before they turned into two cold lifeless marbles, a brief ray of peace and gratefulness shone through them.

At that moment I wished there were a God for cats somewhere who would forgive Midnight for her sins and take her by her paw through the heavenly gates for the duration of her nine eternal lives.

***

Tom Fallon
Rumford, ME

A Walk in the Woods

Walking she and I,
leaves flowering red, yellow and orange,
floating
to the path
along the brook flowing over mossy rocks, we turned,
deeper into the woods
climbing a hill
and entered a clearing
of fallen yellow leaves
circled by yellow leaved trees in white sun light
and
she and I stood
in the glowing unearthly light of creation.

We stood in paradise.

Jane Derbyshire
Tenants Harbor, ME

The Old Cat

She used to rummage in newly turned earth
so warm and soft
now just her little bones

I dug a hole in the autumn and put her body in
so chilly and soft
the old cat, I dug her in.

And presently the spring drops sunshine on the place
so green, so new and soft
And she'll wake up in a seed inside the soil

she's curled and so fine layered in her basket
the earth, sweet smelling and soft
and soon wild lupins will erupt.

***

Gerry Di Gesu
Union, NJ

Fear of Flying

Over capricious sheets of foam
flight I ache to share
feet planted on a sturdy board
the windsurfer's lone translucent wing
grabs the wind—
soars   flies   leap-frogs
across roiling steel-gray seas
racing clouds to the horizon

Sylvia Little-Sweat
Wingate, NC

Silent Prayers at Easter

Still self-quarantined,
Birdsong, sunshine, solitude—
Abide with me—my plea.

Blessed by the sunshine
Birds sing the hymns as God speaks
In the silences.

Jesus, calm my fears
Become my Emmanuel—
God with us—stay near.

In Gethsemane—
May this Covid-19 cup
Pass my lips, untouched.

Near midnight the glow
Of a supernova moon
Dispels deep darkness.

Against the grayness
Of Coronavirus Fears,
Yoshino still bloom.

In morning's first light,
My tulip magnolia
Wears a purple robe.

Mary Ann Giasson
Rockland, ME

Paint Chip Poetry

Filtered sunlight
found in the foggy morning
of a pale vista.

Gypsy love
found in the tapestry gold
of a country lane.

Stardust
found in the cream froth
of a tidal wave.

Serenity
found in the pink harmony
of a floating seahorse.

Blackberry wine
found in the fond memory
of a yellow rain coat.

Twilight
found in the wisp of mauve
of a summer plum.

Crème Brule
found in the yellow marigold
of a harvest moon.

Robert B. Moreland
Pleasant Prairie, WI

Lost in Wonder

Reflections on Winslow Homer's Young Ducks (1897)

Chill of fall in the air, Pierre broke camp
Quebec lake unspoiled, we came to hunt duck.
It is rare to find wilderness this pure,
birch bark canoe glided across the lake.

Bundled up warmly, the morning was damp.
The guide paddled silently this Canuck
who knew the waterways here though obscure;
we could not afford to make a mistake.

Across the bay, the echoing call ramped
up, heard long before we saw them, full of pluck.
A hen and twelve ducklings in tow detoured
in a line across the broad water opaque.

At the sight alone, paused in surprise, tamped
the gun wadding and pondered their bad luck.
For two hunters disturbed their early tour,
readied my rifle and looked for the drake.

The wonder overtook me, God's own stamp
on this rare wilderness possessed by buck
and bear. Rifle down, enjoyed the allure
of creation so fine that my soul ached.

Philancy Comeau
Rockland, ME

A Humble Life

I have six months to live.

When I heard the news, I quivered and quaked. I opened my arms to the warmth of the sun and turned various shades of green, nearly dropping to the ground! Can you imagine being told you have six months to live?

I'm not trying to be elusive about who I am, but I want to draw your attention to the natural world around us: begin to consider what natural wonders you're missing, what you might want to see when you have six months to live like me.

It's not much time, but at least I should see three of the four seasons. I love the garlands of seasonal sights, sounds, and smells that whirl and weave as they travel through time forever connecting the seasons and leaving behind sensations that make them distinct from one another.

In early spring, when the weather is heartless, patches of snow remain in places hidden from the sun, delicate snowdrop flowers pop up through the semi-frozen soil seeking warmth along with crocus and a few other distant plant cousins. As the days warm, daffodil and tulip trains travel across the countryside bringing ribbons of color for all to see.

In spring, with the sweet, sunny summer to come, you can look up to the sky and see green, white, and pink buds of promise dotting the trees. Buds that will burst open in the warmth of the sun to reveal a supple leaf, just as the butterfly bursts from its cocoon. If you will, one work of art becomes another more intricate work of art. Who is the artist? Is it Mother Nature or a supreme being?

All I can tell you is I love trees, and why shouldn't I? I've been attached to them my whole life. Speaking of trees, have you ever considered their leaves? Every leaf is as different as the next and as alluring as a lover.

I love when spring transitions into summer. The days

Philancy Comeau
Rockland, ME

become longer and warmer, like when the passions of young love become the lasting romances of the mature. But, when the heat of the sun prickles your flesh and the sultry air wraps tightly around you, everything droops, including me. All I can do is hold on and wait stoically for the cool evening air to perk me up.

On behalf of tree lovers everywhere, I encourage you to put down your favorite elixir, turn off your cell phone, and walk away from your television. Yes, just walk away. Go ahead, step outside and take a deep breath of fresh air.

Now, that fresh air has stirred your senses, take a look at the leaves that surround you. You may need to cross the lawn or walk down your street to do this, but step up to one of these magnificent plants and embrace a leaf as if it were a friend. What type of edge does it have, smooth or serrated? How about the shape? Is it oval, truncated, or maybe it looks oddly familiar to a tulip? What about color? Is it dark or light green like the inside of a lime? How about purple? While you're at it, check out the veins on the top of the leaf versus the underside. If you walk around the tree, you'll find the leaves vary slightly in color or size, depending on the quality of their surroundings.

Do me a favor and give it a try. I think you'll begin to reflect on what other natural wonders you're missing; what else you might want to see when you have six months to live like me.

Like many of you, autumn is my favorite time of the year. The warm days and crisp nights awaken my senses after a lazy summer of breezy afternoons and the occasional rains.

The change in weather shepherds in the autumn colors that attract people to my hometown of Hope, Maine. Cars and buses loaded with tourists choke the roads and the air. They pay thousands of dollars to come from around the globe to spend time gazing at our hillsides covered with a blanket woven with nature's threads of red, gold, and orange.

I understand why the broad views of our Maine forests

are a major attraction. Few things look better dying than they do living, and one of those things is a tree leaf. Can you think of anything else that turns beautiful shades of red, gold, or orange when it's dying?

Another of the great joys of hanging around trees is watching the migratory birds fill the branches. The slapping of their wings against the air and their constant chatter make quiet nearly impossible. They come and go at will, but they all move on to roost in another tree, in another place, just like our visiting "leaf peepers" who gaze here and there only to leave for places unknown.

I love watching people clean their yards in autumn for the coming winter. They rake leaves and trim bushes and trees, clearing away the dead and ugly.

Do you see Mr. Winslow down there? He's the guy in the red and black plaid jacket, standing next to the bonfire holding a rake. Yeah, him. I heard his wife say that we're expecting strong winds tonight. The kind of winds that will strip trees of any remaining leaves exposing their curves and imperfections for all to see. The lovely Mrs. Winslow told him to plan on spending the day tomorrow raking the yard.

Tonight, death will come. I'll be one of the last leaves stripped from the trees, and without the tree, the fluid coursing through my veins will cease, and I will become one dimensional, void of what is life. I'm happy that I hung on to this branch for so long. It allowed me to tell you about my very short life. It's a story of one of nature's most intricate and beautiful living things; a tree leaf.

Tonight, I'll most likely blow down onto Mr. Winslow's lawn. Hopefully, he will rake me up before the wind carries me into the neighbor's yard. You see, the neighbor uses a leaf grinder to make mulch for his flower garden like a butcher grinding his meat. This loud, obnoxious machine will whirl me around in a vortex of dirt and debris, forcing me through mini-machetes, turning me into unrecognizable bits and pieces. There's something about extending the useful-

Philancy Comeau
Rockland, ME

ness of my life that makes me uncomfortable. As much as I like my distant plant cousins, it's not natural for me to end up as a backdrop for their beautiful flowers.

I find Mr. Winslow's approach much more acceptable as he will return me to my rightful home, the forest floor. He will rake me up and throw me in his bonfire with thousands of other leaves. This is a violent process as well, but we will spark and crackle in our own way, remaining individuals until the end. He'll return our combined ashes to the ecosystem from which we came so that we may fulfill our true purpose, to provide nutrients to those who live beyond us so that they may realize their natural destiny. As appealing as a beautiful garden can be, it's not customary for me to complete my life cycle, insulating store-bought plants from the harsh winter to come.

Well, I must be going. I have to prepare myself for my release from the branch I've called home my entire life, a grand total of six months. If you want to remember me, take a walk in the woods and enjoy the uniqueness of the living leaf.

***

Patrick T. Randolph
Lincoln, NE

Singing Quilters of the Pines

Morning chickadees dart and dance
Among the snow-whispered pines.

Threading the needles of their songs,
They sew patches of snowflake-silence together,
Making a quilt for our winter-worn ears.

Marcia Annenberg
ME & NY

The Tide

Life is fluid like a river..
Streams, eddies, ...people rush by
    our lives—like geometry we intersect
at interstices for better or for worse
    and then the water regenerates
Cycle of life, from
  sky to water and back again...
The children's children
    carry on our burdens
    and our promise
Continuity of broken
    And fulfilled promise
Love like rain
      comes back
Hate like rain
      Turns to clouds
Love and hate intertwine
    In worlds to come...

***

Patrick T. Randolph
Lincoln, NE

Small Sage

Into the wind, into the cold, into the snow;
Body bent forward, skin pierced with winter pain—

Snowflake lands on my nose-drips
A moment of peace into my soul.

Trudy Wells-Meyer
Scottsdale, AZ

Song of Life

*One word or a pleasing smile is often enough to raise
up a saddened and wounded soul.*

— Thérèse of Liseux

Sunlight fills her face, her smile and outstretched hand,
singing in the wind her heart she'd offer to anyone,
a blessing to value this Colorado lady who does
not know the meaning of not loving.

Love and you shall be loved.

They say joy is a choice; this remarkable lady who believes
      in
the good of mankind, she sees stars beyond her sight.
Oh, how I have come to love her joyful embrace
of life, in a growing collection of memories.

A woman young at heart.

Her kindness, a blue-sky Tsunami towers over everyone,
words and smiles touch shoppers in the Mall,—the salon
      —anytime.
Dallas her name finds the music in her world like a bridge
in the sky, a winner in the game of life.

A lady clear of mystery.

Wrinkles don't age, not smiling does—bony hands and
      loving
pink, always a beauty of design walking in like royalty,
      except
her limp curls all but cover her head, a cry for help,
a pleading stare I felt on the back of my neck.

Trudy Wells-Meyer
Scottsdale, AZ

Elegant is her second name.

A resigned bad-hair day would bloom once again, her giant
　　smile
to match, how high her hair should be, how I tried
to hide my cringe, *yes—higher—please.*
Closer to God!

As if it already wasn't.

Every Wednesday she went to the Mall, parading her hair,
　　shop
at her favorite store, long-ago-fashion we'd see once a week,
heads turning, her taste impeccable, clothes and jewelry
that would become mine—*hand-me-downs* with style,

I still wear with pride.

The tide of time has caught up, bygones of yesterday, no
　　more
winter trips for Arizona sun but, twice a year brings us
　　back
to Grand Junction, her home, to find her smile—a smile
the shortest distance between two friends.

The lady with a smile for everyone.

Memories the colors of the desert in the spring, a display of
　　stars,
as a Pharmacist's wife, a cocktail of wisdom and knowledge,
to stay healthy I call, and hear a smile in her voice,
love from a far, a miracle cure on the way.

Kindness delivered surrounded by love.

Trudy Wells-Meyer
Scottsdale, AZ

A belief in the presence of God, she keeps on sailing within
    the
sun, smiles for everyone, the fullness of her joy like a glass
of warm spiced wine for the soul ignites feelings that
are hidden from too many out in the cold.

Where love was never not meant to be.

A hush of surprise, thank God for a daily click on a
    machine,
called computer, only one e-mail away. Dressed in one of
    her
gifts with class—I love them all, I write these words
for a rare jewel, a lady who believes feeling good

starts with looking good.

A smile to follow me to the end of time, illuminated by the
    setting
sun, her way most likely to cheer up someone's day
and before sleep, to make a memory
God wants to keep.

May love guide your life, spread joy and kindness . . .
    Smile.

Cynthia Rainfrette-Barlow
Lincolnville, ME

Grammy's Surprise

My four-year-old grandson, Caleb, was visiting for the weekend and surprised me with a cup of coffee. I woke up early the first morning of his visit smelling the distinct aroma of fresh brewed java. I live alone, so the essence emanating from my kitchen to my upstairs bedroom was definitely alarming!

This is the story of that particular morning. It takes place bright and early on a Sunday. The morning before, when Caleb arrived, he had watched me, his beloved grandmother, fill the Mr. Coffee with cold water, spoon the grounds into the basket, add water and plug in the machine. Caleb was fascinated with the sound of steam and percolating water within the coffee pot. He was ecstatic to see how water magically went through the machine and came out the little hole as coffee. He enjoyed watching the brown liquid dribble in as it filled the glass carafe. This mesmerized the little boy right up until it finished brewing.

"You know, Caleb, this is the best part of Grammy's day," I told him. "The first cup of coffee in the morning."

Being a responsible grandmother, during the process, I reminded my darling grandson how dangerous it was for little boys to make coffee or to *ever, ever, EVER* plug anything into an electrical socket. I also reminded him that he should *never* do so without adult supervision, explaining that his older brother, Zachary, who was almost six, was *not* considered an adult either.

Like a good little grandson, Caleb promised he would not touch the cord, the plug, or the socket until *he was grown up big*, which he and I decided was sometime around ten years old.

For good measure, I also included the microwave, the stove and my computer, along with the vacuum cleaner, the

Cynthia Rainfrette-Barlow
Lincolnville, ME

clock radio and the electric frying pan as needing to be *grown up big* before touching.

Assured Caleb would follow my rules I gave him a small cup filled with his mother's recommended healthy snack of raisins. And because I was Grammy (and his mother wasn't around), I added a handful of colourful peanut M&M's, which Caleb happily consumed first, while watching, of all things, morning cartoons on television. And, since it was Saturday morning, the first morning of his visit and his mother wasn't around, and he *was* at Grammy's house, what more could a grammy do than ask, "Do you want strawberry milk with your Lucky Charms, Caleb?"

***

Early Sunday morning, as far as I could figure, Caleb must have awoken about the time the sun crested the tree-line. It was probably around five in the morning. Knowing the sweet, kind and thoughtful personality of my middle of three grandsons, I realized in retrospect that he wanted to do something nice for his grammy, for he loved visiting me whenever he could.

Remembering that he was not to plug in any electrical appliances until he was *all grown up big,* or use them without adult supervision, he most likely decided he could make his grandmother a very "special" cup of coffee without using her coffee maker. Four-year-olds can be very innovative if given the chance. Oh, and very, *very* quiet as well.

Now, it needs to be established that I am *deaf as a post* and I sleep *out like a light* (both clichés intended), and not having slept with my internal *mother-hears-the-kids-radar* turned on in over thirty years, did not hear my grandson get up and sneak downstairs. Therefore, I was quite surprised to see him standing at the side of my bed in wet jammies holding my favourite blue coffee mug filled with coffee at six o'clock in the morning. (Yes, the child was downstairs in the kitchen, unsupervised for at least an hour. Please do not tell his mother!)

With a smile as big as the sun, Caleb handed me the cup of lukewarm coffee and proudly announced, "I made it myself, Grammy."

I untangled myself from the blankets and sat up quickly, while gently taking the mug from Caleb's little outstretched hands, and smelling the air for smoke. In my calmest voice, I asked, "Did you use the coffee maker?" I awaited his reply, grateful the house was apparently not on fire, grateful he was not electrocuted, and *very* grateful he was still alive and safe. However, I was a bit concerned he hadn't listened to my instructions to not to touch the coffee maker. "Caleb, did you use Grammy's coffee maker?" I asked again.

"No, Grammy, I'm not allowed to, 'member?"

I let out a thankful sigh. He *had* listened to me. "That's a good boy, honey," I said. Then my eyes narrowed. Even the *bestest* grammies can narrow their eyes and get to the bottom of situations, even if they do involve their favourite grandson. (*Sh-h-h.* The favourite part is supposed to be a secret!)

Glancing at the cup again, I inquired, "Did you touch the stove?"

"No, I'm not allowed to do that, don't you 'member Grammy?"

I smiled. "That's a good boy, honey."

"You gonna drink it?"

"Of course I am!" I sipped the tangy lukewarm mixture while little Caleb waited anxiously to hear the verdict on the quality of the coffee he had made special.

I was definitely forced to sip slowly, for I had *never* in my entire life, I mean NEVER tasted anything quite so horrible as the concoction my beloved grandson had so lovingly prepared that morning. In the back of my mind, I wondered exactly what I might be ingesting, having tried not to look at the muddy creation as it passed my lips.

Cynthia Rainfrette-Barlow
Lincolnville, ME

As I sipped, I envisioned dirt from one of the potted plants, dried cat food from the cat's dish, or even pepper from the shaker as probable ingredients. It also had a melted plastic flavour. The last thing in the world I would ever want to do was hurt my little grandson's feelings. So, I smiled bravely and said, "Caleb, I think this is the most *special*, I mean the most *very specialist* cup of coffee Grammy has ever tasted. Thank you honey." I kissed him gently on the forehead, noticing there was a small glob of grape jelly in his hair.

Caleb beamed proudly and climbed up onto the bed, snuggling down beside me. He watched, as I sipped my coffee. (Little did he know his beloved grammy was also bravely praying the wet, soggy Doctor Denton jammies pressed up against her side were wet from tap water and not...

"This is very delicious, Caleb. Grammy might have to save some of it for later."

"No, that's all right Grammy. You can drink it all. I can make you some more."

I smiled, but deep down inside, I prayed I would not die from poisoning. I hoped the water had come from the faucet and not the cat dish. And, I *really* prayed the coffee came from a jar of instant I kept in the cupboard for emergencies when the power went out, and not spent grounds from the trash can, or, God forbid, old dried up canned food from the cat dish. However, from the flavour, I was certain it was instant coffee, figuring by the taste, the amount in the cup to be somewhere in the realm of at least half the jar or more and the odd flavour was grape jelly.

As I sipped, I wondered if drinking the whole cup might cause my heart to explode. On the plus side, I figured the ingested caffeine might be valuable. I could clean the entire house, mow the lawn, wash the cars, paint the trim and stain the deck in one fell swoop! However, as I sipped on, my mind began to race. This *could* be dangerous. I would certainly not want my heart to explode, but better *that*, than ever hurting my little grandson's feelings. However if my heart did explode, I would hate to see Caleb arrested for Grammy murder. What to do? What to do?

Assuring myself all would be well, I decided I would rather err on the side of not hurting my grandson's feelings, so I forced down the remainder of brown liquid as Caleb proudly looked on. I drank right down to the bottom of the cup, until I noticed three little green plastic army men in the bottom of my mug. *Ah ha! That* was the plastic flavour!

This discovery made me smile; the melding of essences between dirt, artificial something or other, and plastic. When I was finished, I crawled out of bed, assured myself my wet grandson was indeed wet from water, and shrugged into my housecoat and slippers. I headed down stairs, with little Caleb in tow.

Downstairs, I patted the little boy on the head, as I stripped off his wet jammies, surveying the water on the floor, the cupboard doors all opened, the kitchen chairs in various spots around the countertops, and the array of dirty dishes in the sink, on the table, across the counters and... how many spoons did the child use?

"You know Caleb this was probably the very best cup of coffee Grammy has ever tasted. Thank you honey!" I once again praised my grandson, as I cleaned up the mess.

His look of pride melted my heart and I wanted to squeeze him. I helped him climb into his clean jersey and overalls, and as I pulled on his socks and sneakers, I did give him a big squeeze and a bigger kiss on the cheek.

I lifted him down from the chair and stood him on the floor, but could not help but ask as casually as I could, "Caleb, honey, why were there three little green army men in the bottom of Grammy's coffee mug?"

Caleb looked up at me, his little hands perched on his hips, and proudly announced, "'Cause it's like on TV, Grammy. THE BEST PART OF WAKING UP IS SOLDIERS IN YOUR CUP!"

Sandra Conlon
Steamboat Springs, CO

Carpe Diem

How shall I seize this day
azure skies and snow clad peaks
shimmering sun splashed streets
words and thoughts bid me to stay.

How shall I seize this day
in winterscape stark and spare
when life's sweet memory
draws me to a quiet place.

How shall I seize this day
in a summer fading flower
the fortunes of each hour
will not come this way again.

How shall I seize this day
shadows passing everywhere
death holds each one at bay
without pretense or despair.

How shall I seize this day
when by some mere happenstance
behold the cosmic dance
stunning luminosity.

How shall I seize this day
yield to its impermanence
once simple innocence
time enfolding blessedness.

Austin Gallant
Rockport, ME

Destitute

Collapsing spectral grotto
Sanctity of dusk
Floor of pulp

Birds want nothing
Man is gone
Moss hangs

Voices of trueness
Feelings of nostalgia
Cold water

All consuming ego
Self destruction
Dead soil

What has come has gone
To take its place an unnerving abode
Where the flow of life no longer gushes

To be alone
Nobody knows
Until—

Cynthia Partington
Dallas Center, IA

Perfect Imperfection

In Memory of Eric

Your advent brought out the good in us
laughter shared, hopeful plans, generosity
I never saw you curling your fingers or wiggling
but felt the warmth of a family together
before you had a name

We see ourselves as strong, able to do all things
if we set our minds to it
until all we give is not enough
some things it seems are not within our power
we are reminded that we are frail, human

Knowing you well is left for a later universe
I feel you too would affirm that life
is for giving, sharing, and dreaming
not for holding on
to the walls we cannot scale

The struggle that was your existence is over
while our struggle continues
and we are left to find other gifts to treasure
there will always be that empty space
you were going to fill

Time lessens hurt, pressing fresher losses upon us
human destiny is a tangle of love and growth
it is not for a lack of loving you that we love again
but that our hearts were meant to love
and that the need to love demands expression in us all

Cynthia Partington
Dallas Center, IA

A minor surgery, a doctor's error
your gifts left unfulfilled
though your waves forever linger
brushing our consciousness unexpectedly
through the years

22 Sept. 1977–17 Nov. 1977

***

Sister Irene Zimmerman
Greenfield, WI

Diagnosis
for Marge, Ph.D

Flood waters are nearing
my front step.

I'm terrified
as I try to decide
what to leave behind,
what to schlep
up the stair
to the attic of my mind
to further explore

before the waters
seep under the door.

Janet N. Gold
Camden, ME

Hibiscus

I pick one flower,
a perfectly red hibiscus,
place the plucked end in water
hoping it will drink and
stay with me for a while,
stay alive though I know
the picking will shorten its time,
has already changed its fate
from coquette to languid beauty.
Longevity is hardly the question now.
Perhaps there is no question;
there is only this looking, looking,
this small remorse that I have interfered,
this sigh for my clumsy human flesh
that steps on grasslings,
leaves footprints in pink sand, in mud,
picks a hibiscus
and only then remembers
that fate surprises us,
picks us from our bush,
our limb.
So I place this perfect blossom
behind my ear
its bawdy pollen-laden stamen
observing me
from the corner of my eye—
here we go together
stepping out
to see what we can see.

Susan J. O'Neil
Kennebunk, ME

Polishing the Past

The first piece of silver I received was a baby cup, engraved with my name and birthdate in elegant script. In its infancy, the cup was banged and battered on the high-chair tray, but it survived and sits now on a shelf in shining, albeit dented, retirement. It survived so long only because it was taken away from me during toddlerhood and not returned to my care until motherhood.

The stages in between weren't kind to sterling silver.

When I was ten, a package arrived with my name on it which was, in and of itself, a thrill. Opened, it revealed a gleaming silver tea service—a generous gift from Aunt Lillian. My mother said, "Lillian has no children, so she's entrusting this to you."

Mother polished the service lovingly, wrapped it in plastic and put it away until I graduated from college. It was then I learned why Lillian had really given it to me. She was sick of polishing it.

Silver custodianship presents a moral obligation. The silver is relentless and unforgiving. It doesn't care whether you like it or not; whether it has any function beyond that of dust-catcher. If you possess one iota of good, old-fashioned Yankee values, you just can't let it go to certain oxidation.

Year after year the tea service and I battled. I'd let it go as long as I dared until a mottled and tarnished guilt would creep over me just as surely as it had crept over the tea service. Then, I'd take out the polish and rub away, cursing my aunt in the process.

Eventually other pieces joined the service, through no fault of my own. My maiden great aunts Dolly and Mary gave me a compote with scalloped edges when they left their seaside cottage for a double room in a nursing home. My uncle from Indiana presented me with a small silver cufflink tray

Susan J. O'Neil
Kennebunk, ME

when he stopped wearing cufflinks.

An elderly neighbor dropped off her ornate porringer as she prepared to enter the local hospital for the last time. Having no family, she didn't want to leave her special piece orphaned, too.

For years I stored my collection in a black plastic trash bag. That was practical for the moves from one studio apartment to another as my twenties led me from Boston to New York; from an advertising career to acting classes to writing, semi-starved, in city garrets as artists are known to do. I moved nine times in one decade, and each time I threw my secret sack of silver across my back. There were lean times when I considered selling some pieces, but didn't.

Later, I married and we settled into the New England countryside. Pregnant with our first child, with everything feeling promising and strangely permanent, I finally unpacked and discovered the rich and soothing properties of silver.

As I awaited the birth of our baby, I polished the silver. As I watched spring flirt with winter, tempting a crocus through a crust of snow, I polished the silver. Waiting, watching, thinking of the givers, I polished the silver. And each stroke became a caress.

Today my silver is on display on shelves in the living room. It gets polished regularly; each special occasion on the calendar is a reminder to take care of my sterling obligation. At the kitchen counter this morning, as I rubbed at Dolly and Mary's compote, I remembered them fully—their voices, their fashions, their pure white summer kitchen where we shelled beans and the latest catch from the sea.

My eight-year-old climbed up on a stool beside me as I rubbed paste around the glinting scalloped edges. "What's that?"

"A compote."

"What's a compote?"

"I'm not sure, but did I ever tell you about Great Aunt

Susan J. O'Neil
Kennebunk, ME

Dolly?"

As her small fingers dipped into the polish, I thought about the day I would give her this silver piece and wondered when her annoyance would turn to love.

***

Sylvia Little-Sweat
Wingate, NC

Alaska

Aqua-marine blue,
Mendenhall's chiseled moraine—
chasms cracking ice.

Along Skagway Trail
bleached bones and broken axles—
Gold Rush detritus.

Fairbanks' river boat
paddles past Husky homestead—
eagles high in sky.

Caribou and moose
roam Denali's wilderness—
grizzlies—hidden still.

Dall sheep dot the cliffs.
Ptarmigans scratch tundra dust—
pink fireweeds blazing.

Denali—High One—
breaks through clouds. Below, rivers
braid the valley floor.

Gerald George
Belfast, ME

Christmas!

Red wrappings, bright greenery, everywhere.
Logs flaming in the fireplace.
Now the family gathers around the table,
the gleaming goose,
mounds of mashed potatoes
steaming under lakes of gravy,
cranberries, celery, olives, squash
waiting on the plates.

Thank you O Father
for thy many blessings,
for our family all together,
for the warmth and comfort
of our home,
for the—

Telephone!

Father rises, strides through the double doors
of the dining room into the hall.

Hello. Yes . . .
Three of them . . . ?
Yes . . . yes . . .
When you find them, hold them . . .
We must find out how they got out.
Yes . . . no, I'm not coming in.

Gerald George
Belfast, ME

He returns, announces:

A matter at the camp.
I'll take care of it tomorrow.
Come, let us rejoice!

Then their feast begins.

Outside,
over the snowy road at the camp's rear
uniformed men track down the missing prisoners,
who beg to be shot rather than taken back.

***

Gerry Di Gesu
Union, NJ

Earrings

Too expensive can't afford them
Although no price is known
Don't belong in this shop of treasures—but

On white satin – created for me
Two triangles of hope and joy
Held by slender silver hooks

Aqua, pink, amethyst
Stones cascading down a waterfall
Reflecting beauty and promise

Of new life and a future
Of harmony, splendor and elegance
For a withered soul

Thomas Peter Bennett
Silver Spring, MD

Spanish Moss

Between the last sliver
    of sunlight
and the dazzling
    blood moon,
a mysterious
    fragrance,
delicate and elusive,
    draws me
into a tangled grove
    of live oak trees...

Ancient sentinels decorated
    with bluish gray
flexuous tresses,
    bedecked with
tiny, fragile,
    cyan-colored flowers.

Like a night moth
    in a gentle forest breeze,
attracted by the
    fragrant essence,
I search for locks of moss
    and gather flowered
strands for musing.

Pat Spiller
Wells, ME

Fare Thee Well

My father was a man of many sorrows who sought solace his whole life long from the triple nightmares of childhood poverty, his father's WWI injuries and death at age 58, and from his own experiences with war in the 1940s.

Sometimes on a Saturday afternoon with his buddies and a bottle of whiskey, I'd hear them talk of war. Their stories brought raucous laughter designed, I think, to staunch the horrors their young eyes saw and couldn't forget. Did my father seek counsel about his war memories, his fears and sorrows? Some vets found therapy helpful healing their post-war stresses but for my father, therapy would be as distant as the farthest star. Not something he would ever do.

But the time of my story is actually late winter, 1986. My father lay in his hospital room, barely hanging on to life, infrequently lucid. He'd been diagnosed with advanced lung cancer five months earlier. Oh, yes, he'd been a life long smoker starting that ugly habit as a young soldier in WWII when cigarettes were dispensed freely by the US Armed Services and the tobacco manufacturers. He got the habit of smoking then and continued for many long years after the armistice of 1945.

My father's illness was terrifying for my mother who lost her mother when she was a child of nine years old. And, though she loved well, and because my father was her whole world, she denied the reality that she would soon lose him to this horrible disease. I felt her phobia around illness took away the opportunity my father might have had to say goodbye to her and to his children. But then, who am I to say? I was the daughter, not the wife. I had my own grief; it wasn't her grief.

Hospice services were offered and would have continued until the end but my mother refused saying she didn't believe

Pat Spiller
Wells, ME

they would be there when she needed them. Her fear may not have been real but it was true in her reality. Though I had different opinions, I was not the decision-maker; I was the daughter and I hadn't lived in their home for many years.

And so my father stayed at home, took treatments of chemotherapy and radiation until the very end when his physician ordered him into the local hospital. We all knew he'd gone there to die. It was beyond sad, for him, for my mother, for his six children.

My youngest sister and I were fearful our father might die alone at night and so decided to spend the last of his hospital stay by his side. Awake, we'd stay through the night until morning; we slept during the day returning after visiting hours in the evening. We watched the nurses come and go, taking his vital signs and taking away vials of his blood. I couldn't understand the need for such a protocol. He was dying; they knew it; we knew it and I expect somewhere, somehow my father knew he was reaching the end of his days on this plane. So why did they insist on these useless procedures?

Early one morning, my father's physician came to the room while we were still with him. I grasped the opportunity to ask if it was necessary to continue taking vital signs and drawing blood. Could he not write an order to stop them, I asked. He looked at me sternly and asked in a terrible voice, so, do you want us to kill him? I was shocked by his cruelty. I had no words. I just looked at him. Nothing came in response save the pounding in my temples. And so we each walked away towards our different ends of the hospital corridor.

Late one night, Michelle and I decided we'd sing for my father. We chose a favorite wartime ballad, one we knew he loved. I was on one side of his bed, my sister was on the other side. Both of us leaning close to my father, we sang softly:

Pat Spiller
Wells, ME

Underneath the lamp post by the barrack's gate
Standing all alone every night you see her wait
She waits for the boy who marched away
And though he's gone she hears him say......

My father opened his eyes, he looked towards me and he smiled a smile that spoke worlds of emotion he might share, if he could. Words of love and longing and loneliness. We sang on:

Oh, promise you'll be true
Fare thee well Lily Marlene
Till I return to you
Fare thee well Lily Marlene.

My father died on the afternoon of the following day. Around his bed were his wife, his six children and spouses. He spoke two final words, the only words he'd uttered in weeks were, *don't smoke.*

He was a man of high energy with a big soft heart. Yes, he was quick to anger but he was just as quickly remorseful. My father was a man with many friends who counted it a bad day if he didn't make at least one new friend.

On the day of his funeral, lines formed inside the funeral parlor and snaked outside and down along the sidewalk: friends, co-workers, neighbors, and acquaintances waiting to say, *fare thee well*, Robert.

Ashley Elizabeth Mitchell
Lincoln, ME

Perhaps

Another birthday has come and gone
Another year wiser?
Perhaps.
That is what is said
Doesn't mean it is true
But at least we get the badge anyway.
I sit here in isolation
Solitude.
Is this how May felt?
Perhaps.
But she made the choice
The choice to live in
Solitude.
I did not make the choice
Did I?
Did She?
Does anyone actually make this choice?
Perhaps.
Whether it is ordered to us
Assigned to us
An idea
Concept.
Could solitude be predestined to us
As individuals of humanity?
Perhaps.
It is something to contemplate while we have a moment
now.
There are a lot of moments to discover now.
Who we are as individuals
To come together
Or to keep dividing.

(continued)

Ashley Elizabeth Mitchell
Lincoln, ME

Discover the truth
Reality
If there are such things.
In the end it is what we make of it
We can rewrite anything
Correctly?
Perhaps

***

Erin Covey-Smith
Freeport, ME

Distance

Each night, when you've washed the dishes
and I've boiled the tea, you put on music,
soft as sunset, haunting as moonrise.
You settle into your slouched couch corner,
and me in my chair, and we read separately,
together.

Before you go upstairs, you hover over me
while I finish my sentence; I stand
to lay my ear against your chest, hearing
what I always hear—a quietly pulsing,
somewhat fraught, but always passionate
universe, that makes sense to me.

Let's not travel too far from each other for too long.
I wouldn't know how to write you a letter.
We hold between us a vast and reverent silence,
made tenable only by the proximity of our orbits.

Mary Ann Bedwell
Grants, NM

Dirty Words:
Words that should never be used in polite society

Abuse, genocide, extortion,
Ridicule, racism, bigotry,
female genital mutilation.

Hatred, contempt, decimation,
Collateral damage,
And friendly fire.

We should never hear these words
Spoken, but if we don't speak
Them, how will we ever know?

What crimes, what inhumanity
Might be hidden
Behind our unwillingness to speak

Words that themselves have
The power, the power to wound,
The power to kill.

Capital punishment, assimilation,
Crimes against or by the state—
Dirty words, words I never want to hear.

Genie Dailey
Jefferson, ME

Entering Hope

The sign flashes by as I drive toward home on Route 17. I've made this journey dozens—perhaps hundreds—of times before, but today the modest DOT sign that says "Entering Hope" takes me down previously unexplored roads. Yes, I'm coming into the village of Hope, Maine, but suddenly those two words have a totally different meaning.

These days, I am continually trying to enter, reenter, and maintain an attitude of hopefulness. Climate change worries me...but electric vehicles and fewer smokestacks give me hope. The cost of electricity worries me...but the potential of wind, solar, and tidal power gives me hope. Burgeoning land-fills and plastic pollution worry me...but public awareness and activism give me hope. Now, pandemic illnesses worry me...but medical research and dedicated health care professionals give me hope. Bullying, name-calling, and insults bandied about by both young people and adults worry me... but here it is harder to find hope. So I make a conscious choice every day to remain optimistic about the *good* in people, and to "enter hope" each morning despite the news broadcasts.

Here in Maine, the towns named after faraway places like Paris, Naples, Norway, Mexico, and China get a lot of attention, including a postcard-worthy road sign listing nine of them. But Maine, like several other states, also boasts towns with uplifting names that reflect the ideals of their founders—Hope, Friendship, Liberty, Freedom, Harmony, and Unity. I like to think that the folks who live in these towns continue to reflect and uphold the ideals and values for which their towns were named. In this, I guess my optimism and idealism are obvious, and I'd like to see more signs that say "*Welcome* to Freedom," "*Welcome* to Liberty," or "*Welcome* to Friendship"—and *none* that say "You are now *leaving* Unity" or "You are now *leaving* Hope."

Andrea Suarez Hill
Jonesboro, ME

Color of Time

We lose
sunset in horses eyes,
brown reflecting pools,
that show the sky
    in grassless pastures...

shriveled leaves that crack
beneath my feet,
save the crimson oaks that
    unravel one by one
        hanging on 'til snow comes...

my breath rises,
 a white flash
with a skeletal shadow
stretched in l'heure bleue,
 as the last light splashes
    tree tops ocher at four...

 an untimely dark
 laid on the land
with arbitrary unreason
  makes afternoon night
and steals a gentle season.

A. M. Clark
Cushing, ME

She edged her garden
for Lyonelle

with a bold, clean line,
pulled up the weeds
and hauled them away,
then gave to the soil
a most potent drink.

No one applauded
that hot, windless day,
but down at the roots
was a party of sorts
and the hovering sun
in its own silent way
was laughing and smiling
on what she had done.

***

Steve Troyanovich
Florence, NJ

for Bootsie Barnes

already the melancholy tones
of morning's blue syncopation
stagger toward the notes
of your voiceless saxophone...

Sandra Conlon
Steamboat Springs, CO

On Forgiveness

Something about forgiveness
strips the soul of pridefulness,
softens grief and loneliness
eases the torment of despair.

Something about forgiveness
purifies feeling and thought,
heals the sorrows of the heart,
restores a sense of balance
when we see us as we are.

Something about forgiveness
creates a thinning of desire
to overpower the other,
releases the soul ensnared
longing for a simple gift
of kindness everlasting.

***

Sylvia Little-Sweat
Wingate, NC

Hope

Redbuds and dogwoods
Epitomize Eastertide—
Life, Eternal Life.

David S. Holt
Jacksonville, FL

Sailor Wannabes

"I just love sailing," said Carole as we crossed the Robert Moses Bridge to Fire Island and saw hundreds of white sails spread out on Great South Bay. The scene reminded me of a piece of navy blue fabric dotted with little white triangles.

"I do too," I replied. "How much have you sailed?"

"Oh, not much, but I love being on the boat when it's leaning over a little as it slides through the water and the wind blows my hair back. Do you know how to sail?" she asked.

"I had an adult education class in Smithtown years ago, but I didn't have much chance to practice what I learned. Do you know how?" I asked.

"Not really, one of the guys I used to date explained a few things, but I never actually did anything. I thought my job was to relax in a new outfit and look cute and adorable like the pictures you see in magazines."

That may have been our first conversation about sailing, but it was definitely not our last. On our honeymoon we watched sailboats on Lake Champlain, the St. Lawrence River and Lake Ontario. In Toronto we joined a group for a sunset cruise on a large two-masted sailing vessel. The next summer, while vacationing on Maui, we had a charter sail on a 36' sloop.

The following year we moved to a small community named Sayville on the south shore of Long Island, and it placed us within 600 feet of the Great South Bay. This location gave us more contacts with sailing. Our neighbors had a sailboat, we could walk to the town dock and marina, and we could lie on the beach and yearn for a ride on those boats that sailed past us. We also discovered that some of our friends had sailboats, and we jumped at every invitation that was offered. We were becoming convinced that we could sail

David S. Holt
Jacksonville, FL

and forced to admit we had to stop talking about it and actually do something.

"Look at this," Carole announced. "The Coast Guard Auxiliary is giving a boating safety course, why don't we sign up?"

"Aye, Aye, Matey," I saluted.

"Hey, I could be the captain," she said.

"Yes, dear," I quickly replied.

At the first meeting we paid $20 for the six classes, but we bought only one workbook to share. The instructor, Captain Jim, looked as though he had been around the world with Magellan from the looks of his dark leathery skin that was deeply creased around his eyes and mouth.

"How many of you own boats?" he asked. Of the twenty people in the room three hands went up.

"Any sailors?"

One of the three raised his hand.

"Okay, this course is all about safety for both power and sailboat owners. I want you to know the laws, the regulations, the customs and the courtesies of operating your boat safely. But—there are people in boats who don't know these things, and they can hurt you."

He continued, "I assume you all used driver's licenses to get here tonight so you're familiar with the concept of, 'right of way.' Men have been sailing a lot longer than they've been driving, and the concept comes from sailing. The problem is, whether on land or water, a person can have the right of way, but he can also die for it. The job of a captain of any vessel is to avoid an accident, whether he has the right of way or not."

That was our introduction to boating safety, and we were eager beavers. We gave up TV time to study our book and answer the questions, but we found that it was harder to share one book than we thought. One was using it when the other wanted it too. Finally, after learning about radios, charts, landmarks, buoy systems and, "right, red, return," we had to face our in-class written exam.

"I'm so confident that all of you will pass this test that I've made up course completion certificates for everyone," Captain Jim announced at the beginning of our last class.

"Sure, that's easy for him to say," whispered Carole. "What if I fail?"

"Shhh!"

Captain Jim added, "There are no time limits for the test, so just relax and enjoy yourself. Turn in your booklet when you finish, have a seat and we'll call you when we've scored your test."

As I worked my way through the test I was feeling confident and looked to Carole on my right and smiled. She smiled at me and then looked down at my booklet. Automatically, I leaned forward and curled my right arm around my exam, a response ingrained by many years spent in classes taking and giving tests. She looked stunned, as if I were accusing her of cheating. Her smile vanished, her body stiffened, and she bored in on her booklet.

Finally, when we had handed in our tests and they were corrected, we were called up to see our scores and receive our certificates. As we walked out of the room I said, "I got only a couple wrong. How did you do?"

"Hah! You thought I was cheating, didn't you? I'm not telling my score. I got my certificate and I passed. That's all you'll ever know."

Although it was a warm spring evening, I sensed a distinct chill in the air.

In a conversation with one of her co-workers, Carole was reminded that he had learned to sail in the Outward Bound program years ago and now was a certified sailing instructor.

"Mike, how about teaching Dave and me to sail?" Carole asked.

"Sorry, I don't do couples," Mike replied.

"What do you mean?"

"I mean I've had some very unpleasant experiences trying

David S. Holt
Jacksonville, FL

to teach husband and wife teams. I've seen yelling and cry-
ing, and one couple didn't pay me."

"Well our case is different. How many years have you
known me? You know what I'm like, and I can tell you that
Dave is very even-tempered, doesn't get upset easily and in
three years of marriage we've never had an argument."

"I don't believe you."

"It's true. You can ask my mother. She has lived under
the same roof with us in two houses and she's never heard a
peep."

"It's against my better judgment, but okay. I'll give you
some dates tomorrow."

Mike had a 24' Catalina sloop with a retractable keel that
was very serviceable for the shallow waters of the Great
South Bay. At our first meeting it was obvious he was an
affable guy, and we hit it off right away. We boarded at the
dock on the canal in his back yard and he used the 15 hp
outboard to motor out to our training area.

Mike began by introducing the names of the parts of a
sailboat.

"It's important that you're thoroughly familiar with the
terminology because if the weather suddenly changes, the
captain must get his commands to the crew quickly, and the
crew must know what the commands mean and act accord-
ingly."

The terms were overwhelming at first, but as we began to
use them in sentences they made more sense. On that first
day out the best part was Mike let each of us take the helm
and we had the thrill of guiding the boat toward some distant
landmark. He demonstrated, "coming about," and Carole
and I successfully executed that maneuver as well.

Five Saturday morning lessons went well, and we gained
a little more confidence each time we went out. We even
sailed up close to the Robert Moses Bridge and became one
of those little white triangles to motorists crossing over to
Fire Island. Mike coached us through many tasks, from low-

ering the keel board and raising the sails to jibing and getting out of, "irons." He conceded that perhaps we were an atypical couple as he never heard unkind words exchanged through any of the tasks that frustrated us.

On our sixth, and last, class, we performed most of the skills we had learned, and then Mike asked, "What would you do if one of you fell overboard?"

Carole's immediate reply was, "We don't allow that on our boat."

"Seriously," said Mike, "for the kind of sailing you're thinking of, it seems like it can't happen, but it can, and you must have the rescue tools to deal with it."

"I'd throw her the life ring," I volunteered.

"Well, that's a start," said Mike, "but who picks her up, the next boat to come by?"

"Of course not. I'd bring the boat about to get her," I said.

"That's right," Mike replied. "You must know how to get to the person in the water, so now we'll practice the Man Overboard Drill."

He brought out a good-sized buoy with a rod sticking through it. On the short end of the rod was a weight, and on the long end was a small banner.

"Throw the man overboard, Dave," Mike directed.

I did as I was told, and then Mike shouted, "Man overboard."

"Don't lose sight of the man in the water!" he yelled.

"Ready about? Hard alee."

The boat came about quickly, and we approached the buoy on the weather side, slowed and Mike reached over, grabbed the flag end of the rod and pulled the buoy on board.

"Okay, Dave, throw him in. Carole, your husband just got knocked into the water. What do you do?"

"Man overboard!" she yelled.

"Good! Dave, for this exercise you'll be a passenger who goes up to the bow and reaches out to grab the survivor when the boat approaches.

David S. Holt
Jacksonville, FL

"Ready about? Hard alee," Carole called and brought the boat around. However, as she tried to reach the buoy, the boat was off to the side by 12–15 feet and I couldn't reach it.

"Come about again," said Mike.

Carole managed to bring the boat about and headed for the buoy from the opposite direction, but again she couldn't get close enough. "Hey, I could be dying from hypothermia out there," I yelled.

"Oh, shut up," she snapped. "Why won't this boat go where I want it to?"

"Try it again," said Mike.

As the boat missed the buoy for the third time, I called out, "I'm drowning, I'm drowning!"

"Good, I'm ready to leave you there," Carole spit.

After about 15 minutes Carole brought the boat alongside the buoy so I could pull it aboard.

"Well, you did it," congratulated Mike.

"Yes, but..." was Carole's reply. Then she said to me, "And you were no help at all. I had enough pressure without your attempts at humor."

"Okay, Dave, your turn," Mike said as he threw the buoy overboard.

"Man overboard!" I yelled.

"Carole, you go up to the bow this time to pick up the buoy," Mike directed.

"Ready about? Hard alee," I called out.

The boat came about nicely, and I got a good sight on the buoy flag and I came up to it quickly. However, as I was trying to ease off the sail and slow down, I lost sight of the flag and then I heard and felt a big "clunk."

"Darling," Carole said ever so sweetly, "You just ran over me."

"Oh @#$%^&*," I said as the buoy popped up astern. I brought the boat about, came up alongside and Carole pulled the buoy over the rail.

We sat down with Mike, he looked at us and then shook

David S. Holt
Jacksonville, FL

his head. "I don't know about you two. You may not argue, but I think there must be some repressed hostility in there. First she's willing to let you drown, and then you run her over."

He may have been skeptical, but we were ready to buy a boat. But that's another story.

***

Austin Gallant
Rockport, ME

The Chasm

The sun sets,
a somber glow,
an afflicted sky.

A portent of demise,
yet all endures,
in abstractions.

Aimless hearts,
ebbing into the chasm,
of desolate prospects.

Forever lost,
forever abandoned,
forever a shadow.

Deborah LeFalle
San Jose, CA

View from My Throne

They appear one by one
in no specific order
in varying gradations of gray
Tiles beneath my feet are cold.

puffer fish, aka blowfish
big ball of water and air
poisonous secretions
smart defenses to keep predators
from having nice meal

Winkie Guard in busby hat
on command from Her Wickedness
marches in unison
spewing baritone chants of
elongated vowels

the drinking gourd
bright asterism against darkened sky
follow it to freedom
follow it to hope

ancient inscriptions on
stone, papyrus, parchment, wood
telling stories of life
for future generations

volcanic crater
I wonder when the last eruption was

Deborah LeFalle
San Jose, CA

Frankenstein's
piecemeal head
with dramatic stitches
holding face skin together
a monster of an experiment

baby elephant
hooting owl
paw tracks in dirt
whose are they?

Assemblage suitable for framing
Tiles are warming now.

***

Patrick T. Randolph
Lincoln, NE

Half-Price Bookstore in the Afternoon

I start with the best
And absolutely the worst
Pick-up line ever;
The best because it's
Direct, the worst because it's
Always overused.
"SO, do you come here
Often?" I ask.
Her eyes roll,
She gives me a smirk.
I take her hand and
Listen to her laughter grow;
"You nut!" sings my wife.

Denise Pendleton
Belfast, ME

Out There

He goes out to the woods in the long
Afternoons of a weekend, and in spring's
Late light he goes in the evenings as if
Called to hold some meeting there.

I've seen him crossing the field
With shoulders bent and head down,
And from his hand the chainsaw nods
Its silent assent before vanishing
With him into the woods.

What calls to him doesn't speak to us
Who live with him in the house he built
To keep the outside out of. The house
Our mother keeps tucked around us
He shrugs off, a man holding everything
He ever needed inside.

F. Anthony D'Alessandro
Celebration, FL

...Bop, I Don't Know Brown!!!...

Behind a wrinkled brow, my eleven-year-old grandson, Brock, said, "Bop, I don't know brown."

I battled quivers sparked by my insensitivity after I'd casually asked Brock to hand me a brown envelope. His shrugged shoulders reminded me of his color blindness. I hugged my grandson, while struggling to mask watery eyes, and apologized. Then I yanked the brown envelope from my files.

For years, I'd relished Brock's gazelle-like athleticism. I photographed his honor roll ceremonies. I thought that I totally understood the boy but his comment about "brown" hurled my emotions into free fall. I had not considered his color vision deficiency.

This stirred a memory. I had mentored 500 dynamic and quality teachers in two states. When I observed interns, I visited each classroom several times a semester. I recall one map-skill lesson presented by a student teacher. On desks blanketed with white sheets of paper, students were asked to color and label states.

As my intern lectured, I saw two grinning boys working together. The smaller boy pointed things out to his friend. The taller boy cleared his throat repeatedly and kept drying his hands on his shirt. Suddenly, my intern's supervising teacher leapt from her desk shouting, "Do your own work!" Color drained from both of the boys' faces.

Although my student teacher was not involved in the classroom teacher's confrontation, I suggested that she diplomatically speak to the teacher about the incident. Based on the chatter regarding color that I'd overheard, I suspected that the boys' cooperative work related to color blindness.

I imagined the heart-pounding angst buffeting a child's struggling to identify color. Perhaps the student experienced

F. Anthony D'Alessandro
Celebration, FL

the same stranglehold of stress I had felt when I'd lost the admission ticket to my SAT Exam last century?

Before our next observation, my intern teacher said that she had talked to the boys, and one knew of his pal's struggle with colors and decided to help.

I asked if her teacher was aware of the problem.

The intern said that when she told the teacher about the color deficiency, the teacher checked the student's record and confirmed it. She apologized to the boys, adding, "I don't have a heart of stone."

Color blind youngsters are affected in other ways besides academics. At a basketball championship game involving young players, Brock experienced difficulty distinguishing the baselines of the courts used in tournament play. Out-of-bounds lines looked nearly the same color as the playing floor to him. In this sport, costly court changes are not necessary, just a recognition of possible color issues for some players and ensuring that these lines are more recognizable.

We've heard and applauded the success stories of former President Clinton, Howie Mandel, and Mark Zuckerburg climbing to the pinnacle of their careers, despite this visual problem. Put yourself in the place of a young student with color-recognition difficulties, however, and imagine the increased pulse rate, fluttering stomach, and sweaty palms when pressured by these visual issues.

Why not make life easier for children who say to grandparents, "Bop, I don't know brown!"

First published in *Orlando Sentinel,* January 8, 2018.

Erin Covey-Smith
Freeport, ME

March Poem

Books that remain closed too long
must get so tired of looking
at their facing pages. *(But light, too,*
falls, you know.)

Wes is sad today, folding in on himself.
I know how it is: I want a small and nested space,
fur-brown and warm, to keep the chaos at bay—
the one place chaos does not like to be kept.

It laps its undeniable, Janus-faced wisdom
around our edges: there is no in or out, no open
or closed, no scared or sacred, exclusively.
We are all fissured.

Maybe this is how it is:
we keep catching each other
hand under hand, down and down
through the unknowable depths
with the raindrops falling all around.

Down and down, like sedimentary drift
to the ocean floor. Even as the rising waters
eat the islands, new land bubbles from the broken
ribs of the broken earth. We are not done, yet.

The snow has melted now in all but patches,
and I remember, getting in my car one day
with a sideways glance at the still-sleeping yard,
I planted bulbs last Fall: daffodils and tulips.

Karen E. Wagner
Hudson, MA

Sand Castles

Plastic buckets make
sand castles
with sea shells
as windows,
fortified walls
surrounded
by seaweed-filled
moats stand high
against the enemy.
The stuff kid's
beach capers
are made of;
'til the hours
of the day tick
away, erase
the world
to start afresh.

My sculptures too
have feet
of sand
to stand not
for eternity
but until the rising
of the next tide.
Sandman
throws his
shadow deep,
reaching out
a pudgy finger
to touch the

(continued)

Karen E. Wagner
Hudson, MA

lapping waves.
He holds the
answer to "Why
build here?"
"Because
it's on the edge
of graciousness
with a beauty
of the moment,
and no
forethought
of things
to come."

Because I am
growing old,
ageing is my
nemesis.
My body
resembles the
weathered piers
more each day,
washed in the tide,
battered by waves,
worried by barnacles;
as I regard my sagging
body buttressed
by a spandex suit, I
remember that child
with the plastic
bucket and
like her, joyfully
greet the recasts
of melted sculptures
the waves lick away.

Robert B. Moreland
Pleasant Prairie, WI

Awakening

With the biggest yawn, the old man stretches
feeling sap run up from his misshapen toes
firmly anchored in the verdant black loam
out to the tip of his arthritic joints.

For a century, he has stood his guard here,
a sentinel on this once broad prairie.
Cornfield now yielding its crops in season,
progress gone by, he stands gaunt and ageless.

Born from an acorn hungry squirrels missed,
his brothers succumbed to the farmer's axe.
Cousins in the adjacent field still stand
while the farmer plows around burr oak isles.

Long awaited warm spring day comes at last,
the first blooms show, nascent yellow green leaves
envelop his aging body once more;
back bent, centenarian in this field.

Red tailed hawk alights his upper branches,
scans the view as field mice and rabbits hide.
Red wing takes a lower branch, head back, sings.
Buckthorn bushes crowd his roots down below.

When he was young, draft horses plowed this field
and black Model Ts drove Delany Road.
Men flew with the birds above him while he
watched all of their children grow old and die.

Robert B. Moreland
Pleasant Prairie, WI

Patriarchal burr oaks have no real choice,
firmly anchored, they cannot move away.
New houses will come and brethren slain, fall.
Our *progress* will end his long life at last.

***

Steve Troyanovich
Florence, NJ

in the shadow of lullaby
for Elizabeth

> *Now in your shadow—my shadow rests.*
> —Boleslaw Lesmian

upon a mantle
gathering lilacs and dreams
your hair cascades
into the quiet murmur
of slumbering shadows

wrapped in crystalline moonlight
drowsy ouds pluck
the melody of your repose

in a temple of moonbeams
and unfading spring
snow leopards guard your sleep

...softly now hug tightly
every drifting star
you are tomorrow's refuge
grasping the caresses of your eyes

Brenda E. McDermott
Searsport, ME

Passing Through Searsport, Maine

Searsport woos me
as the winter sun settles
over Penobscot Bay
glittering the high tide with
earrings of silver loops.

East on U.S. Route One,
mansions of former sea captains
and ship builders, in different
styles of architecture, some embellished
with carriage houses, others built in
high Greek-Revival style line both
sides of the highway.

Pure New England churches
reflect energy of honorable
buildings, as well as the
Penobscot Marine Museum, which
shelters artifacts of a vital time
and harbors a rustic flavor in its walls.

Moose Point State Park offers
an expansive view of the bay,
and reveals blue winter shadows
on fresh snow. I can almost see
ghosts waving their fog-colored hands
as I exit the park.

Roe Chiacchio
Camden, ME

Fifty Shades of White

During wintertime in Maine, we are surrounded by leaf-less trees, frozen lawns and barren land. But within a day, Mother Nature will suddenly sweep in to beautify the terrain. After her snowstorms, look out and see a virgin landscape of snow where there was once a lawn. A sculptured white scenery unmarked and untouched by humans or animals.

With admiration, I scan the carpet of snow containing cut diamonds that sparkle and glitter as the sun sweeps across the land. Nighttime brings a distinct illumination. The moon-light enhances the snow's brightness as darkness escapes the night.

I am mesmerized by winter's beauty. The snow is of the purest white. I feel a deep longing to be in her world, to be close to her and snowshoeing brings me into her fields and forest.

Snowshoeing is a free style sport. I can go anywhere, any time of day and night. I can travel up a hill, down a ravine, around a fallen tree or under a fence. The land before me tempts me to explore her without barriers. The trails don't have to be groomed. What I see before me is where I can roam. I am limitless to create my personal destination.

The snow is soft and giving with each step I take in my snowshoes. The latest storm dumped two feet of fluffy padding to trek on. I sink twelve inches, which makes walk-ing a chore and every now and then I sink deeper, up to my thighs. Being stuck in snow is like frolicking in a playground. I'm not worried about getting bruised or bumped or hurt because the snow acts like cotton balls, cushioning my falls. When I'm lodged deep in snow, I dig around me, roll, climb out and then lie on my back to watch the clouds drift by, happy to be in this quandary.

The snow is unblemished, pure and shadowy and her

Roe Chiacchio
Camden, ME

whiteness glows from within the shaded woods. As I wander, tones of natural daylight produce images along the ground creating fifty shades of white. Alluring, hypnotizing and enchanting, Mother Nature demands my attention to notice her beauty and I am captured. *Look to the left, look to the right, look up and look behind you*, she whispers, as displays of ethereal images from the trees, shrubs and rocks surround me.

Within the forest, the varying colors of white give contour and depth to the land. As the sun moves across the sky and peeks into the woods, shadows change in shape, size and hue. The forest floor comes alive with dancing figures along my path.

I peacefully meander, listening to the sounds of snow-covered trees and shrubs cracking and snapping, trying to dismiss the weight of the snowfall on top of them. Branches are hanging low to the ground creating tunnels for me to travel through in a crouched position. The forest behind my house contains eastern hemlock trees, a favorite food of the animals living here. Having the branches close to the ground makes it easier for deer, moose, porcupine, mice and fellow friends to dine in deep snow. This is nature taking care of her occupants.

I travel alongside a frozen stream, stepping around the debris of fallen trees and broken branches, knowing the deer will use this trail later in the night. I have given them a path to wander on, thereby saving their energy so they don't have to do the exhausting work of breaking trail in deep snow.

Henry Thoreau believed there is a benefit in walking. "Me thinks that the moment my legs begin to move, my thoughts begin to flow."

Snowshoeing, like walking, has a liberating effect for my mind. When I am outdoors, I am living in the moment. This allows me the time to distance myself from the stressors of life. I am creating a space away from my world of family, work and commitments to feel the spirit within me. And in

Roe Chiacchio
Camden, ME

this space, of being between both worlds, I find the truth of my life.

When we are in nature's environment, our brain shifts its focus towards being fully engaged and present in our existence. The secret is finding our footing in her space and learning to listen.

Next time it snows, take a walk into the woods and there you will find fifty shades of white.

***

A. M. Clark
Cushing, ME

Winter Wind

Our tumult love is up there in the branches
of the firs that might blow down tonight
and lose their brittle, fragrant, frozen lives
and then who knows what may O yes
befall us here below, writing in our laps,
drinking icy vodka as the winter world
in cold collapse becomes the end itself,
a cataclysm hard and real down through
our heavy roof and windowed walls, all miles
and miles and miles beneath an almost here
beside us, almost smiling moon tonight...
then mellow down our fears with talk of bed
and sleep and all the strangest dreams we'll
surely have beneath this constant roaring.

Patrick T. Randolph
Lincoln, NE

Depends on the Road—A Wisconsin Ballad

I once asked you what kind of music your soul likes—

Unlike any answer I'd ever heard before,
You said, "It depends on the season,
And the road I'm taking."

Tonight, while driving home—
I imagine you on a mountain valley road,
Windows down, smiling—an old folk song
From years before your parents were born
Follows your car down a winding curve.

In the rearview mirror—an image of you
Dancing with your father in the living room—
A late evening father-daughter ball.

Sound of your mother's applause next to an open
Summer night window—curtains clapping in the breeze.

Peggy Faye Brown
Gray, ME

Calming Our Busy Minds

In my opinion, one of life's nicest pleasures is to unplug from technology and curl up with my cat and a good book. We are inundated with a constant stream of information throughout the day and sometimes, it is just too much for my introverted self. The news of the day is often scary and repeated over and over again. Looking back at a news broadcast of a month ago, I find it interesting how that scary news is often no longer mentioned at all since there is a new panic of the day. When you are a worry-wart like me, it is just too much. Fear kept me from attending an annual event I enjoy due to not wanting to be in a crowded auditorium. Was that truly necessary?

It is time to escape from society and relax my mind. I ignore the housework, turn off all electronics, and sit in my rocking chair. My cat finds me and curls up on my lap. Reading at the ocean would be nice but since it is March I'll stay cozy and warm inside my house. The rain pelting against my window lulls me as the ocean waves could do. In my quest to read old books again, I take *1984* off my shelf which I read during high school in 1982 when it seemed far-fetched. After skimming a few pages and noting some parallels to today, I find it is not a source of relaxation. I put it away and select a soothing book by Maya Angelou, my favorite author.

Our brains need opportunities to relax, process, and refresh. Finding calmness, kindness and compassion in our daily lives can help. I was reminded of this while watching the movie about Mr. Rogers who many of us have fond memories of watching on television as a child. His voice was gentle and he slowed everything around him by truly listening and being present in the moment. Maya Angelou's voice was also gentle and calm and her quote, "Be a rainbow in someone

Peggy Faye Brown
Gray, ME

else's cloud," certainly applies to the personality of Mr. Rogers. This is a good reminder of how we can help each other when stressed out by the news of the day.

Many of us Mainers go outdoors to calm our busy minds. Since we've recently turned our clocks ahead, we are nearing the time of peaceful long walks or relaxing times fishing and swimming in our lakes and beachcombing at the ocean. Recent conversations with people who come from hectic cities remind me how lucky we are to wake up here each and every day. Seek out your favorite way to relax and recharge your mind, whether by being in the woods, doing yoga, running, fishing, or reading a good book.

My cat suddenly leaps from my lap and reminds me it is his supper time. I glance at my analog clock to discover how much time has passed during my mini escape from reality. As I close my book, I notice the storm has ended and a beautiful rainbow has appeared outside my window. Feeling refreshed, I put my book away. I will start making dinner, but I'm not turning on the evening news.

Jeanine Stevens
Sacramento, CA

At the Pic N' Pull

It's all fenders, radiators and engines
in a heap; heavy blocks sit alone,
most of the paint gone—rust
a part of the charm.

Before computer diagnosis
you could make your own small repair,
spend an afternoon with uncle's Nash,
                      brother's Chevy.
In our old Buick, we drove to picnic grounds:
checked cloths, chicken and pickled beets.
On Mother's Day, a longer trip
to the cemetery, made better
if we had time and money to stop
for pork tenderloins on the way home,
if not, white bread, Spam
and a Thermos of ice water
                      by a shady stream.

Now, on Saturday afternoons,
young husbands come after lawn mowing
car washing, a needed respite
from their new domesticity.
They can no longer afford trips to Vegas.

Near a slumped Pontiac, grease-stained ground
resembles a brown hedgehog pelt.

I gather a clump of dandelions
to see if I still
                      have butter on my chin.

Janet N. Gold
Camden, ME

Sea Lavender

Limonium carolinianum

Her territory:
the essence of temporary,
the uncertain, beaten, worn
and ever-moving, ever-changing breath
where sea and moon
exchange their greetings.

She thrives,
indeed can only survive
among shore rocks and marsh grasses,
her roots anchored
in soft and spongey sea mud.
The air she breathes is cold and salty.
Her taut, thin stems,
wrapped in seaweed
and the papery remains of crabs,
branch into spikey statements
of tiny blue-gray flowers,
sprays of pale delicacy
that hint at her tough tenderness.

She's weathered a lot of storms,
has many tales to tell.
But she saves them.
And when all the other flowers
are dead or dormant
and it is winter
and we look for warmth and stories,
there she is,
reminding us
that the tide advances

(continued)

Janet N. Gold
Camden, ME

and the tide recedes,
so send your roots down deep
and hold your head up high.

***

Sylvia Little-Sweat
Wingate, NC

Nova Scotia

Halifax lighthouse
shrouded in Peggy's Cove mist—
bagpipe elegies.

Sydney's Cape Breton
touts tall sculpted violin—
Gaelic gigs and jigs.

Anne of Green Gables—
revenant of Charlottetown—
Prince Edward Island.

Quebec City's crest
reached by steep funicular—
tall ship masts below.

Gulf of St. Lawrence—
whale in tandem cruising ship
spouting baleen spray.

Montreal's bright flags
wave Canadian farewells—
Maasdam docked in port.

P. C. Moorehead
North Lake, WI

Broken

I picked up the deadfall and gazed at it—
dry, sere, dark—myself.

How did it become so drear,
so dark, so fallen?

I gazed at it and lifted my eyes.
There was light. There is light.

The deadfall doesn't have to be; I see that now.
The deadfall mustn't be.

The dead branch can be broken,
and new life can arise.

***

Grief

I didn't want again to enter that far land.
Yet, here I am.
It is too familiar, too painful.

Grief's presence destroys me—
and creates me.

I am old; I am new.
I am here.

R. Craig Lord
Cushing, ME

Lip Newsome

Lip signaled for the left hander in the top of the ninth. At least that's what everyone thought, but when nothing happened, Sanchez the shortstop ran out to the bull pen to tell them. Left field was a bad sun field at Walker Park that time of day, and if the bull pen had been watching the game, they might have had trouble seeing. That wasn't the case. Standing on the mound, Lip started to shake his head, making that muffled noise, exactly like a man with duct tape over his mouth. By the time Fenton got there, Lip was beet red and a small amount of foam had formed in the corner of his mouth. He grabbed Fenton by the collar and pulled his face right up and stared into his eyes. This continued until the ump broke it up. Lip released his hold and walked into the dugout. Fenton, God bless him, struck out the side and the Rose City Balers won 7–5. It was the only time I saw Lip get mad. The rest of time he never said a word.

Billy Maguire, Russ Simon, Ron Whitten and I were sitting in the corner of an Outback Steakhouse in Culver City, Tennessee. The table was covered with empty pitchers, dirty napkins and plates with chicken wing bones. We had just finished our season in the Mid America league and were having a few beers together before everyone went their own way. It was my third season for the Triple A Culver City Blackrocks. I hit .285 that year with 18 homeruns. Not bad numbers, but never good enough. I knew the pain in my knee was never going to go away. As I looked at the end of my run it occurred to me that my career, while chock full of oddities, characters and strange occurrences, had one thing that I would never forget. I had played baseball for Lip Newsome. The boys wanted to know what it was like.

"Are you talking about Ricky Fenton? The guy with the Brewers?" asked Ronnie Whitten. Whitten was a big strong

R. Craig Lord
Cushing, ME

kid who was going to stay in the minors until he could hit a curve ball.

"No," I replied. "It was Timmy Fenton, I think he's a high school coach in Alabama somewhere."

"How could Lip manage without being able to talk? I mean he couldn't yell or nothing," added Billy Maguire.

"Think about it. Just cause he couldn't talk didn't mean he couldn't manage. Every day he would make out the lineup card. If you were on it, you played, if not you didn't. He always made the right move and if he didn't, who would you complain to? The guy couldn't talk. You would never have made it Maguire. Lip would have run you by Memorial Day."

Maguire would have made it, though. He was Lip's type of ballplayer cut from his high school team, he had made it this far on his hustle and hard work.

"I remember one day late in August I was on the bench. Wendell Cranston was pitching for Birmingham in the Reds organization. I believe that he got called up that September. Top of seventh, two outs and we get three guys on. Lip comes down the line and hands me a bat. Now you guys know Cranston, he's a big lefthander who throws real hard, and I was kind of enjoying my day off. I was also about 0fer lifetime against the guy. So, Lip hands me the bat and holds up four fingers. Now as you might imagine, Lip had a whole series of signs that he used with the pitchers, the tugged sleeve, the tweak of the nose, a tug on the ear, and he had a whole 'nother set of signs for the hitters. For instance, if he was calling for a bunt, he would fold his arms against his chest and throw his head back and stare into the sky. We just called that sign the snore, looked like he was falling asleep. One warm Sunday four batters in a row bunted before the third base coach realized what had happened. Anyway, in all those signs nowhere to my knowledge did there exist the four fingers sign."

"He wanted you to take a walk, it's simple," stated Russ Simon. Russ was fresh out of college. He was considered one of the smarter guys on the team. Took the cerebral approach. His father Bill Simon had a long professional career with the Dodgers and Russ had pitched four years at San Diego State. Russ had the pedigree, but he pitched great until someone got on base. Then that he fell apart.

"He was looking for the long ball," added Whitten. "He wanted four runs."

"I thought about that too. Except that Cranston was such a good pitcher. I had no reason to believe that I could go yard against the guy. I was sure that Lip wasn't expecting me to."

"Whatdya do?"

"My career as you know is filled with watershed events just like this one. In the past I'd always taken the route that ended in disaster. I was determined to succeed this one time."

"Whatdya do?"

"I figured a walk would work just fine. What ever happened after that would be up to someone else. The first pitch was in the dirt. I knew that because it kicked up a cloud of dust otherwise, I never saw it. Ball one. The second pitch was another fast ball down the middle, I swung and missed. The ball was in the catcher's mitt when I started my swing. I stepped out and looked in the dugout. My teammates were up on the rail clapping and shouting encouragement. I squinted, back on the bench there was Lip holding up four fingers." I got up from the table and grabbed a rolled-up menu and took my stance. "I dug in real good, crowding the plate as best I could. Cranston missed with a curveball on the outside corner. The pitch looked pretty good from where I stood, and Cranston agreed. He stepped off the mound and glared in at the ump. I hoped he wasn't getting angry, but he was. The next pitch was high and tight, the perfect pitch to turn and take in the back. I baled and flopped in the dirt. Ended up in the fetal position next to home plate. I got up, brushed myself off and dug in a little less than before. 3–1 a hitter's count if there ever was one. So, I looked for a fastball

R. Craig Lord
Cushing, ME

down the middle. It was. The ball cracked hard in the catcher's mitt. I stood there somehow paralyzed with the bat on my shoulder."

"Full count now. Here's your moment of truth." Maguire stood and topped off everyone's beer.

"I know." I thought about stepping out, but why prolong the kill. Besides my feet felt like they were glued to the ground.

"Had to be a fastball comin." Simon stated the obvious. "You had to know that."

"I did and it was. Cranston reared back and let loose with that heater that by the end of the summer would be buying him a new car."

Life in Triple A was cruel. You were either on your way up or on your way down, and if you weren't on your way up, you were by default, on your way down. I had stayed here in baseball purgatory for three years. Guys that got the call to the majors were celebrated; guys who got sent back were mourned. It was RIP for me.

"Called third strike?" asked Whitten.

"No, I got it. Not quite square on the barrel more out on the end, I put a swing on it though. The ball jumped off the bat. The crowd roared as the ball drove towards the right field stands. Just when it looked good, it started to tail cutting towards the foul pole." I held my pose. The menu wrapped around my shoulder.

"Foul or fair?" they said in unison.

"Long enough, but foul by about ten rows." I looked out to the mound. Cranston was rubbing the new ball down staring back at me. He was going to make this personal.

"Had to be another heater on the way." Maguire caught the waitress's eye and signaled for another pitcher. "I saw where Cranston pitched last night. Got a seven pitch save."

"Yeah, I saw that too," chimed in Simon. "He's in the Pennant race."

I took a couple practice swings with the menu until they

were paying attention again.

"The next pitch was a heater down the middle. I caught it off the handle, fouled it back, and the bat broke in half. The barrel going halfway to the mound. As I walked back to the dugout Lip met me at the steps. A bat in one hand, four fingers showing on the other hand."

Lip was my first manager in professional baseball. He was wiry in appearance with very angular features. His hair was black and peppered with grey. His eyes were cobalt blue. If I had to describe him in one word it would be leprechaun. Without speaking, he taught us everything. I learned the proper way to run the bases, field a ground ball and throw to the right base. All of which was accomplished by lots of pointing and grunting, but mostly Lip physically demonstrating each move. We worked at it until Lip gave us the safe sign. His way of telling us good job. I never saw him after that year. I was on my way up. He wasn't rehired when the ownership changed.

Time was out as I dug in again. I signaled the ump that I was ready, and he pointed at Cranston.

"Here comes the end of the story," joked Maguire. "Swing and a miss."

"I think he's got old Cranston worn out," proclaimed Simon. "Ball four on the way."

"Time for old Uncle Charlie. The curve ball!" added Whitten.

"Well boys, the fourth swing was the best swing. And the ball cleared the 404 sign in straight away center field. And four runs were put on the board."

"That was just what Lip wanted. You did it!" Maguire stood up and began high fiving his buddies.

"It was what Lip wanted. I rounded the bases and ran to the dugout where I was mobbed by my teammates. Backslaps and high fives all around. Down at the end of the dugout there was Lip holding four fingers up on each hand and dancing like a Philly Mummer on New Year's Day. As I

R. Craig Lord
Cushing, ME

reached the end of the line, Lip put his arms around me and
he whispered in my ear.
    "Now that's what I'm talkin about!"

***

Minal Mineva Patel
Portland, ME

I Saw That!

You look
As if you're going to collapse.
Into a pile.
Of bones and flesh.

Let me gather you up
Into my arms.
Before you crumble.

Don't worry,
I'll put you back together.
And I'll let you go.

Someday.

Robert A. Impallomeni
Camden, ME

Jeremy

Planted on the park bench, she continuously shifted her emaciated body as the uneven wooden planks made comfort impossible. She pushed her greasy dirty-blonde hair out of her eyes and stared across the playground. Rusty chains holding empty swings twisted in the intensifying breeze. Swirls of dust and light trash swept around her. The blowing dirt crept into her nose and mouth, its smell and taste acrid. Sniffling into a tight wad of tissues, she sounded near to hyperventilating, and coughed in barks as foul mucous dripped onto the back of her dry tongue. Her look insinuated an age far older than her thirty years.

But none of this penetrated the protective outer shell she'd constructed over time. Her focus was directed at the now abandoned Victorian buildings across from her, outside the park. Exuding an aura of despair, a lonely emptiness. It was as if they sensed their fate.

The childless merry-go-round rotated in short jerks, nudged by the same wind that battered her creased and cracked faux-leather boots with dead fallen leaves. Migrating ducks deserted the shallow near-frozen, ink-black pond for better parts unknown. She shivered in the threadbare cotton coat that looked far warmer when drooping off a thin wire hanger at the *Goodwill.* Pulling it tightly around her jutting shoulders, she blinked rapidly to forestall her inevitable tears.

Everything here was drab and dismal, sepia and gray toned, devoid of color and joy. The bright paint that shimmered off the Victorians in the summer, dulled like a dimmer switch cranked down several notches. Warm tears now dripped onto her chilled cheeks as she reminisced about sitting on the same bench when the park was imbued with life; when everything, every single thing was different. Crying had

Robert A. Impallomeni
Camden, ME

become like breathing, near constant and out of her control.

She remembered those elaborate, ornate buildings when the future was full of possibility and positivity, when families filled the wide inviting porches, barbecuing and laughing, harboring not a clue that it would all end soon. Their lives too would be altered in ways they couldn't imagine. They were as carefree and oblivious as she'd been then. Had she known what was to come, she'd have relished every second.

A twenty-five-story glass and metallic monolith would rise, and replace the empty Victorians once bulldozed to rubble. Families displaced, discarded in the name of progress. Forced out, told to move on, embrace the change, not dwell on the past, get over it, accept that it was meant to be, believe it was God's will; all words and phrases she'd come to detest. Nobody could know the hollowness she felt in the pit of her stomach every single minute, whether awake or in the throes of a nightmare that did not end.

She struggled off the bench. Her muscles ached and fought to stay put. Glancing at the park one final time, she turned and marched towards the highway. The answer to her pain was right there all along. Her pace increased, she held her head high and for the first time in months she smiled then stepped from the dirt onto the pavement, and continued forward, ignoring the blaring horns, the tire squeals and the shocked screams.

Jeremy would be cradled in her arms again soon.

Jerry James Rempp
Reasnor, IA

Entreaty

Higher Nature
We are of elements the same
Our being resounds with nature's harmony
Do you know that? Can you feel it?
Ever do you hear the chords roving
the constant hills, singing to our selves
secluded in the ageless mist
in the breath we both inhale
shared in common lungs
driving the single heart of our
spiritual being, weeping at goodness?
A sweeter lullaby than imaginable
rocks the cradle 'til we sleep
Amen

Lower Nature
Aye, but not as with you, observing one
Nor do I desire the aloof and
abstract portals of divine sense
That self-awareness that beholds refined
from the highest branch of self
I go passion's length apart from pondering
Seldom do I observe the rarefied
That anxious pause flutters disconcertingly
I am grounded in the midst of our selves
I throb, content with the pulsing of
our brain's stem
It is of me I sing
Amen

Jerry James Rempp
Reasnor, IA

Higher Nature
It is of thee I also sing, and to
the light above our shoulders
above our heads—very high
in the branches, and still above
beyond the zenith
swept still farther
'til words of visual delight fail
and we bathe in its cleansing wonder
Amen

Lower Nature
Why bother me with light?
Too much of light! You dally in its
presence as if it were a saving grace
I know the place; I find it in the morning
but I am done with it by eve
withdrawing from its presence
There is delight apart from light
Do not interject me with your light
I am other than disposed
Amen

Higher Nature
I am for both of us with light
Remember, I am you; we are the same
But believe with me in light, whatever it is
It delights before it burns
warms before it sears
It is the glow of sense, reason, conscience
definer of hillside and valley
the shadowy evidence of beyond
Know our limits; know the light
I rest the matter of light
Amen

Jerry James Rempp
Reasnor, IA

Lower Nature
So soon! Delight raptures me
What value such beseeched righteousness?
It only spies upon the natural man
and drives its righteous wedge within
the conscience, confounding reason
I hold it in contempt; the natural is my lot
The noble lioness is benign of instincts
both suckling—and killing prey
Amen

Higher Nature
We are both born loyal unto virtue
You take our glory from the natural
but fail to go the distance
Our naturalness is veiled in pride
to spare us sting of blemish
I am aware, for both of us, our nature
is beyond our thoughtlessness
Beyond awareness, I can tell you nothing
until the next cloud-full clap
bolts a newborn shank of brilliant light
But I shall observe for both of us in good
conscience and reason; I shall be the
sentinel of our singular soul
Amen—and Amen

Sally Belenardo
Branford, CT

In Darkness Found

Only the Sun has no shadow,
sending light in all directions
until it strikes impediments:
the worlds revolving around it,

all creating cones of darkness
behind them in space, where stars are
discovered, a moon gleams, and Earth
has always her shadow of Night
to turn to for slumber and dreams.

***

Gerry Di Gesu
Union, NJ

Winter Clouds

Bitter black layers try to suffocate those below
the pewter mass beneath struggles to catch the wind.
Slate slivers reach slowly toward the west
as alabaster wisps ease toward a horizon
eager for the healing rays of a winter sun.

Then I realize
strength can only come from my core
and rise.

Peggy Iannella Grubel
Lubec, ME

Impaled

Lily waited at the steps when I drove up. Winston lay at her feet.

"Let's take a walk." She raised her voice to be heard over the chatter of birds congregated in the mesquite tree next to the driveway. Her words sounded normal and in charge, so like the old Lily that I did a double take. Three weeks ago, Dr. Kramer gave her a new medication, hoping the drug would be more successful than the previous two. Since her diagnosis a year ago, Lily's memory had faded more rapidly than any of us anticipated. Would this new drug slow the onslaught?

"Come, Winston," she said. The border collie sprang to his feet, his eyes fixed on the three inches of bare skin below my cropped pants.

"Winston's going with us?" I asked.

"You'll be fine," Lily snorted. "Just don't walk like a sheep."

I sidled up to Lily and matched my gait to hers while we tramped down the hill into the desert and breathed in the hint of damp earth, evidence of the spring rain that morning. I studied Lily through sideways glances. She looked the same as she did four days earlier when we met for lunch. She'd washed her hair, an improvement from the dull tangle before, and she'd combed it. The sunlight brought out the natural honey highlights. At forty-eight Lily remained striking. Lately, one needed to search beyond the mismatched clothing and uncombed hair to glimpse her beauty.

Did her husband Jack suggest the cleanup or did she decide herself? Why did I analyze everything to the nth degree? "You think too much," Lily used to scold me. Now, Lily couldn't think enough.

My toe caught on a rock, and I pitched forward. Lily's arm reached out to steady me. "Whoa, Nellie Bell." We laughed at

Peggy Iannella Grubel
Lubec, ME

her reference to the jeep from the Roy Rogers reruns we watched as kids. Winston edged closer to my heels, eyeing me as if I was a recalcitrant sheep but faded away when I picked up the pace.

Her Roy Rogers memory was still solid. I pictured Lily's memories as skeins of yarn. This past year many of the shorter strands knotted, causing her to forget an increasing number of people, names of everyday objects, what day it was, where she stored her pots and pans, and what she said ten minutes earlier. Yet a few of those strands spanning four decades, remained intact.

Lily pointed up ahead. "I'll show you where I've been trimming." We turned from the gravel path into a wash lined with palo verde and cottonwood trees. Winston alternately glided ahead and behind us. Sometimes only the black and white plume of his tail appeared.

The wash narrowed, and I drew my arms close to avoid snagging them on the cholla. The common name for cholla was jumping cactus. A person needed only to brush against the cactus, and the stickers sprung into clothing, embedded in skin. When enough of the hooked thorns penetrated the flesh, whole branches broke off, further entangling the victim. I glanced down, remembering my childhood brush with jumping cactus, how Lily calmed me while she and her father plucked out the thorns with needle nosed pliers. The remaining stickers lodged so deeply that it took months to finally work themselves out. I still wore a bracelet of tiny scars around my right ankle.

Stepping into a depression, my foot twisted. In the narrow space Lily marched ahead. She turned around and laughed. "For crying out loud, do I need to hold your hand?"

I stopped to catch my breath and glanced up the steep banks of the wash. "I hope you know where you're going. How much farther?"

Lily's dark eyebrows furrowed, like storm clouds sailing across the sun. "Of course, I know where I'm going." Her lips pinched together. Abruptly, she turned and marched on.

The wash twisted around another bend. Lily located footholds and climbed up the side. Her movements were still sure-footed and agile. I scrambled after her. When I caught up with her, Lily punched my arm and grinned at the way I kept my eyes glued to the ground. I wanted to avoid tripping again, but also to check for snakes.

Rattlesnakes ventured out in the springtime. Although I never spotted a rattler on Lily's property, Winston was bitten by one a few years ago and almost died. The snake bite occurred before we noticed any overt signs of Lily's illness, but did clues lurk even then?

During those weeks after the snake bite, Lily showed up for our Saturday lunches pale with dark blotches under her eyes. She apologized for her inability to hold up her end of the conversations. "I'm so tired I can't think straight. With Winston so restless at night, I'm up with him five or six times." Lily never recovered from that time. Those sleepless nights extinguished a flame in her, and when it rekindled, the flame flickered instead of blazed.

"It's up ahead." Lily pointed to a copse of mesquites creating a canopy over a clearing in the desert undergrowth. A bench stood in the shade with a bucket of trimming tools underneath. Lily sat, absently kicking the bucket with her heel, and patted the bench. "Sit down before you trip again." After digging a hollow in the dirt, Winston circled and flung himself down.

I settled next to Lily. We were silent while we took in the Santa Catalina Mountains. The fresh redolence of the cut creosote branches permeated the breeze. Lily had clipped the dead branches from the ironwood, mesquite, and palo verde trees, and trimmed the desert bushes. The difference was subtle. This shaded area felt more open and airy. Lily's trimming allowed the desert spring to manifest. With lower branches gone from the palo verdes, the deep green of their trunks popped out. The rest of the desert looked cluttered

Peggy Iannella Grubel
Lubec, ME

and faded.

Lily pointed to a dead ironwood. She had sculpted its branches so that the tree resembled a tall, old man bent over, one branch arm swung forward, and one behind.

I laughed. "It reminds me of your dad."

She tilted her head. "I wondered why it seemed familiar."

This sculpting was Lily in her element. The talent for transforming nature into art evolved into her landscape architecture business. She had a similar talent with people. She saw through the dead wood cluttering those close to her, drawing out their essence. I witnessed it with Jack and her children, and with me.

Lily drew up her knees. "I love it here." Her arms spread to include the desert and mountains. "It's so..." The familiar quotation marks appeared above her nose.

"Peaceful?"

"Yes. Peaceful." She went on. "How's Alan these days?"

"Fine. Fine. He's on another new project, so he's home late. I miss his cooking. I'm eating a lot of Lean Cuisine."

"You don't cook?" Lily faced me, one eyebrow cocked.

"No, I don't cook." I felt like a stone had dropped into my gut.

"How's teaching going?" Lily asked.

"Pretty well. I'm on spring break this week." This conversation had played out almost word for word last Saturday.

"So, what's Alan up to lately?"

Everything in me wanted to say, "I just told you, Lily." Although I knew better than to point out her memory lapses, I failed to tamp down the doses of anger and shame that flared up inside me. It wasn't her fault that plaque filled her brain. Somehow though, the disease felt like a betrayal, and I often struggled to distinguish Lily from the Alzheimer's.

She jerked around to face the wash. "What's that noise?" At first, I only heard the birds. Gradually, I separated one bird cry from the rest. Lily leaped up and sprinted down the bank into the wash. I followed.

Peggy Iannella Grubel
Lubec, ME

"Oh no!" Lily pointed to a cholla. Catching up with her, I glimpsed gray wings flapping in the thorny branches.

"Cactus wren," Lily whispered.

The bird's chirping sounded like screams. Stickers pinned its head sideways and circled one eye. Each time the bird struggled it became further impaled. Within seconds both wings spread out against the branches.

"What ... how did it get stuck?" My mouth was dry, and the walls of my throat squeezed to a slit. Cactus wrens built their nests in cholla. What caused this bird's home to become its execution chamber?

"Oh no oh no oh no." She wrung her hands. "Don't stand there. Help me!"

What could we do? We had no needle nosed pliers on hand. I forced myself to look at the bird. Shock already clouded its eye. "I think he's too far gone."

"No." Lily shook her head. "No. We're going to save him." She searched the ground and knelt to pluck two dead branches from underneath a creosote bush. "Here, try to get him out with these."

"Lily, even if we get him out, we can't remove all the thorns."

"Just try!"

I grabbed the sticks and brushed my hands down their lengths to remove dead leaves, feeling the creosote's sticky sap on my palms. I stood frozen, holding the branches. The bird shrieked, its curved bill opening and closing, but its struggle had lost some of its energy. The bead of its eye bore through me.

Lily pushed me forward. "Do something." Her hands flew to her ears while she shifted from one foot to the other. I had never seen her so agitated, not during childbirth, not even when her mother died.

I bit my lip and stepped forward, feeling Lily's breath, hot on the back of my neck. I lifted the sticks over the bird. Taking a gulp of air, I raised one of them and swung it down-

Peggy Iannella Grubel
Lubec, ME

ward, breaking off a branch. I beat the branches until a nest of broken cactus arms encased the bird. The wren remained attached to the cholla but only by stickers against stickers, meshed together like Velcro.

The bird stopped shrieking. Its chest rose up and down, and the eye surrounded by stickers still stared at me. I crossed the sticks, making a platform underneath the bird, and wrenched the branches from the cactus. I laid the wren underneath the bush, still cocooned in its nest of thorns. Winston moved forward to sniff, then trotted back to Lily.

She knelt. "You've got to get the stickers out."

"How, Lily? How do I do that?" I wiped sweat from my eyes, seeing up close the black eye strip, the gray, downy feathers underneath pinned wings.

I fingered the broken end of one of the cholla branches framing the bird, noticing an inch of green, devoid of stickers. With my thumb and forefinger, I tugged while anchoring the tangle of limbs with one of the sticks. The bird and cholla branches jerked sideways in one synchronized motion. I tugged harder. The bird's face puckered. After several pulls, a branch broke free from the wren's head, leaving a circle of ruby dots.

Piece by piece, I removed the branches. Without my glasses I had no idea how many thorns remained. Glasses were beside the point. It was impossible to remove the stickers without pliers. I shifted my body to shield the bird from Lily. "Let's keep him under this bush. Maybe he'll recover enough to fly away."

"Did you get all the stickers?" she asked.

I nodded.

Lily backed away. "But what if a coyote comes? Or a snake?"

"He's hidden under the bush. They won't see him." The old Lily wouldn't believe this story for a second.

"Well, okay." Lily rubbed her palms on her jeans. Her lower lip trembled when she smiled. "Maybe we saved him,

Karen."

We trudged back through the wash and up the hill toward the house. Neither of us spoke.

***

In Lily's kitchen I heated the water and steeped the tea. Winston flopped under the table, head resting on Lily's foot. The afternoon seemed to have brought a temporary truce between the dog and me. New clouds rolled in, and we listened to the rain while we sipped our tea. I lifted my cup, letting the steam curl over my face and closed my eyes. The cactus wren burst out of the blackness. Would the bird stay dry under the bush? My eyes jerked open. I shifted my legs, knowing I lacked the will to go check.

Lily turned from the window. "Don't you love a good rainstorm?" I watched her face, searching for a flicker of memory from the past hour.

Before the rain stopped, I made my excuses to leave. Winston looked up, but didn't leap to his feet to herd me to the door.

"See you Saturday," I said.

"Have a good week at school," Lily called as I drove away. My hands gripped the wheel.

***

For reasons I couldn't explain, I kept the bird incident to myself. When Alan asked about my day with Lily I only said, "Fine." Did I feel guilt in doing so little for the bird? The old Lily would have done so much more. Or was my silence due to shame for lying to my friend?

The bird haunted me the rest of the week. Sitting on my patio, I thought I heard its scream amidst the grackles scrabbling atop our back wall. A glimpse of gray on a woman's blouse in the supermarket called up the image of the bird's

Peggy Iannella Grubel
Lubec, ME

wings splayed on the cholla. Each night the incident unraveled scene by scene while I tossed in bed. On one of those nights an idea fluttered into my thoughts and took hold. It was the kind of ridiculous bargain I made as a child: if I avoided all sidewalk cracks on the way to school, I'd receive an A on my math test or my mother wouldn't find something to scream at me about when I came home from school. This time I bargained that if, by some miracle the cactus wren recovered, then Lily's new medication would work.

In the following days I couldn't shake the thought, although I tempered it with an element of reality. I knew the drug would not cure Lily, but if it staved off the rapid unraveling in her brain for a year, maybe two, that would be enough of a miracle for me. I scolded myself even as the idea raised a tiny flag of hope. Back and forth my two voices parried. What if the bird was gone, I argued, how would I know whether it was carried off by a predator or flew to freedom? I knew this idea was magical thinking, but once the hope pinned itself to my mind, I didn't let it go.

***

I fidgeted the following Saturday while Lily and I lunched at El Chorro. The bird never came up in Lily's attempts at conversation, and for the second time since Lily's diagnosis I felt grateful for her defective memory.

After lunch I kept the engine running when I parked in Lily's driveway. The appearance of Jack's old BMW reassured me.

"Don't you want to come in?" she asked as she got out of the car.

"No. I have a slew of papers to grade before Monday. I've procrastinated long enough."

"Okay." Lily hesitated. "When will I see you again?"

My smile felt pasted on. "Next Saturday. Like always."

Lily waved. "Have a good week at school."

Peggy Iannella Grubel
Lubec, ME

I waited until she went inside before driving around the bend to park on the side of the road, then cut across the desert until I found the wash. Recognizing the toe holds, I climbed out and searched for the cholla with broken arms. Today the breeze tickling my face only carried the dry smell of dust.

I recognized the creosote bush first, spotting the sticks lying nearby. I bent to peer under the bush.

The bird was gone.

I held my breath. Did the bird recover? Fly away? No signs of a predator. No tracks or scattered feathers. Giddiness bubbled through me. And hope. I chuckled. I'd drive back to Lily's, trigger her memory of the bird, and add a happy ending.

I turned to leave. When I stepped to the side of the bush, a smear of gray caught my eye from a nearby cholla. The bird lay pinned at the top of the cactus, wings once again spread. The sun had bleached the ebony eye to white.

I stumbled through the wash, no longer caring about snakes.

Karen E. Wagner
Hudson, MA

Searching for Sea Glass

Disguised beside rusted bottle caps
and scraps of lobster traps,
my scavenges save many pieces that stayed
embedded at the bottom of the bay
until this last storm scoured them away.

Discarded pieces of glass
once bottles, plates or flasks
served their purpose and been tossed
crushed in the rages of waves, lost
to the depths of the sea
washed up in the sand,
where they wait for me.

Among the cattails and the seagrass
lay the colored shards of treasured glass
that have been sea salted
and buffed to last
a millennium or more
ground lightly upon the ocean floor.

My search for these frosted chips,
scrambled as the surf heaves and dips,
to salvage pieces of a splintered childhood:
those cut-loose days plied sand and driftwood
into games that would adapt and endure
until we players yearned for more.

Karen E. Wagner
Hudson, MA

I look for abraded chunks of memory,
scuffed and flaked as battered glass,
through debris and reeds of inlet beach
where few other treasure hunters reach
sift out my hidden nuggets to
refashion them for native accessory,
on my brown skin the story is worn,
glass pieces and hair beads adorn,
gives me back the whole morass
of childhood reassembled.

***

Take These Hands

Take these hands and
remember what it's
like to hold them in
the blustery days of Winter
when wind
whips our cherry cheeks
and fox run cold with
prey to lair.

Remember what it's
like to hold them
when Spring withers
the snow and
the first crocuses
poke their
heads through the
frost-crusted earth.

Karen E. Wagner
Hudson, MA

Remember what it's
like in our Summer of
peaches, wet and sticky,
when dandelions
are abundant,
bunnies munch on
clover and we giggle
at their antics.

Last of all think of
me in the Autumn when
cancer steals you
and our dreams
dissipate into the ether of
never-to-be and I'm left
holding onto wisps
of everything
we could have been.

***

Genie Dailey
Jefferson, ME

No Escape
A haiku in two verses

I squirm and I twist,
Eyes shut and burning; it's just…
Inescapable.

No matter which way
I lean, or get up and move,
Campfire smoke follows.

Carole Cochran
Boothbay Harbor, ME

Oranges

Here I sit, with a steaming cup of coffee, in my cozy and comfortable home, looking out at the sun sparkling on the harbor. My little world here in Maine is safe, secure, and I relish my good health. Memories bubble up about my childhood.

It is close to Christmas, and my thoughts return to my parents, and the struggles that they had as children. I saw none of that growing up, as we had a happy home, an excellent education, gifts around the tree. Each Christmas was a ritual: my Aunt Freda would read *The Night Before Christmas* from a big picture book; the adults put us to bed gently. They toiled into the night, setting up a tree, arranging the garden under it, with a Lionel train, miniature houses, snow on their rooftops. The gifts were taken out of their hiding places and scattered over the living room, waiting for us to see them the next morning.

My brother and I always woke up early, prodding Mom and Dad to hurry up. The descent down the stairs began, with Dad in the lead in his red plaid bathrobe and Daniel Green slippers, followed by Mom and my brother, then me at the end, straining to see what was below. We did this *every* year, and that ritual was the biggest gift of all. *That* is what is seared in my memory, not what was in the wrapped gifts. (The one exception was the coveted wood table and chairs for my dolls.)

My dad liked to talk about *his* Christmases spent on the farm, with his three brothers and one sister. They had limited financial resources, many mouths to feed, and animals to tend. One of Dad's uncles had moved away from Virginia to Baltimore, found a good job, bought a home, and married a lovely woman named Emma. They had no children, and wanted to share their abundance with my dad's family on the

Carole Cochran
Boothbay Harbor, ME

farm.

Very few people traveled by car from Baltimore to Virginia at that time, so trips were made by ferry. If Uncle Eddie and Aunt Emma could not make the trip, they would send gifts in a big barrel. And what my dad remembered to his dying day was the joy he felt when they met the ferry and opened the barrel. One year it was *oranges*! Enough for all of the children to share, with some left over for stuffing with cloves, putting in fruit cakes, or curling and drying the skins. Aunt Emma was transformed, in my father's eyes, into a special Santa.

I now recall these memories of my father, to keep them alive for me and for my family. When Dad was living the last few days of his life, he asked me to find a picture of Aunt Emma. I put it in a fancy gold frame, placed it on his bedside table, and he sighed with delight. Bringing joy to a child is a wondrous thing, and to have that child remember it until his dying day is even more wondrous.

So what I remember best at this time of year is the joy of our Christmas ritual, not the gifts in fancy packages. And what my dad remembered best was the gift of love, represented by those oranges.

Sally Belenardo
Branford, CT

In the Moment

See the little rabbits, wild and brown,
leap across the lanes and roads of town
to browse on lawns of grass and clover
before the sunsets soon are over.

See them in the moment they are there
nibbling on the sweetness of spring's fare,
for, when rabbits from safe burrows roam,
there are evenings when they don't come home.

***

Birdfeeders

Hungry the Dove with its mournful song,
hungry the Jay in bright feathers blue.
The wrath of winter bitter and long,
we offered them seed as best we knew.

But God made the Hawk with talons strong,
knowing the Hawk would have to eat, too.
We'd come to grips with kindness gone wrong,
and our good deed was something to rue.

Steve Troyanovich
Florence, NJ

lullaby of shattered cradles

This was I,
* A sparrow*
I did my best,
farewell.

—William Carlos Williams

today i watched
a sparrow
perched in early spring
its voice blanketing
a surrounding coldness

i thought of Keats and beauty
awakening tenderness
in a place without warmth

from an embracing cradle
of some other time
i dreamed of things
that could not be...

the little sparrow
continued to sing:
nothing...nothing
...nothing is real

Elizabeth Lombardo
Walpole, ME

Frances and Marian

Prologue

My name's Marian, and I'm a geriatrics nurse at St. James' Assisted Living Center. I've been Frances's personal care nurse since the start of the new year. I'm not telling you this because I need to keep a record—the patient log is HIPPA protected anyway. I'm not telling you because you need to care. I know you have your own dead or dying to look after as it is. I'm telling you her story because I need to remember it, because her story will be my story one day, and I'll feel better about the end if I know what's coming.

Hope

When you're old, you can say just about anything. You're grumpy and senile, and you probably won't be around long enough for the person you're insulting to hold a grudge. Frances is no exception. I've spent a solid hour today shampooing and styling her hair in preparation for a family party.

"Almost done there?" Frances nags me for the third time in three minutes. "I'm not getting any younger here."

"I know, my dear, but you *are* getting more beautiful by the second. Here, look at this," I reply, releasing the curling iron from her wispy grey hair and passing her a hand mirror. "What'd ya think?"

"Tut, tut," she squawks. "People don't know how to do their best anymore. Just call it good enough." She feels around the back of her neck, practically pulling apart the curls I've tried so hard to fabricate out of her short, thinning fluff of hair.

"Is there something I can do to fix it?" I ask patiently. "I know I had a hard time at the bottom there."

"Oh no! It's good enough!" Frances declares. "Besides, you've already taken forever. Michael will be here any sec-

Elizabeth Lombardo
Walpole, ME

ond. But you know," she continues, her sea-blue eyes now trained on me, "you should practice curling the back of your hair. You'll get better at it, and you'll look a lot nicer." I swallow my laugh and thank her with all the appreciation I can muster.

"You know," she continues, fixated on my appearance, "when my sister was in nursing school she wore a uniform with a little white cap. Her hair was always in a bun and stayed in place the whole day. She wouldn't have *dreamed* of seeing a patient unless she was neat and looked presentable."

"Ah," I sigh, "those were different times, weren't they? Thank goodness I don't have to wear a uniform though, right? Then you wouldn't be able to tell me what you think of my outfit every day." I try to sound more cheerful than sarcastic, but I still earn a scowl from Frances as I help her into her jacket.

I have Frances ready to go early. She is sweating in her jacket, but won't hear of taking it off. "Where is that man?" she whines. "He said he'd be here at 5:30." She looks at the silver watch encircling her wrist.

"It's only 5:34."

"Well then, he should be here by now!" Frances exclaims. She shifts impatiently in her chair, as if being forced to wait is a personal insult.

"Who should be here?" A voice rings out as a tall, middle-aged man enters the room, his jolly expression melting Frances's frown.

"Well, there you are!" Frances says, lighting up. "We've been expecting you!"

"Here I am," says her son-in-law, bending down to hug Frances. "How's she been?" he asks, straightening up.

"Just ducky," I reply, a smile on my lips. "She's looking forward to getting out for a bit."

"That's right, that's right. Now let's get going!" Frances commands, returning to her imperious self.

Elizabeth Lombardo
Walpole, ME

"Alrighty then!" Michael concedes. We transfer Frances into her wheelchair.

"I'm going out to do some errands, but I'll be back to put you to bed, okay? You have fun," I say.

"Oh, don't worry. I will!" Frances exclaims, a twinkle in her eye.

***

I come to a realization at the drugstore that evening. I've stopped to look at hair dyes in the cosmetics aisle, Frances's assessment of my looks still fresh in my mind. I know that my face is betraying my fifty years, and my once dark hair is showing more than a little grey. *But what's the point?* I wonder, looking for the right color amongst the decadent sounding shades of chocolate mousse and deepest coffee. *Why do I bother delaying the inevitable fade into grey? It's gonna happen sooner or later. Why even bother curling Frances's hair? What does an old lady care about her hair anyway?*

These questions dance through my mind as I locate my old standby—dark chestnut. I grab the box with its promise of more youthful looking locks when the truth hits me. Hope. Hope is why I go through the messy process of dying my hair every six weeks. It's why Frances demands her hair to be done up as best I can. We go through life, knowing that death is at the end. But it doesn't have to be right now. There's no reason to give up hope—to stop trying, stop living. No, we might not be the prettiest, and we may not be long for this world, but we are here, and we hope to be noticed. We hope to be the best we can be, that something good awaits us around the corner if we just keep on keeping on.

Joy

Frances has been having a rough morning. She woke up disoriented and unsure of her surroundings. Then she received a devastating phone call from her favorite nephew,

Elizabeth Lombardo
Walpole, ME

saying that he would not be coming to visit during his family vacation—he and his children were going to Disney instead. This prompted a solid hour of lamentation and crying, which necessitated a breathing treatment—all before lunchtime, where the dining room just served her least favorite macaroni salad. Now that we've sent away the macaroni salad, untouched, I'm wheeling her back to her room for a bit of a rest.

"How 'bout a nice little nap, Frances?" I begin, wanting the rest for myself more than anything else.

"How 'bout a nice little nap, Frances?" she mocks in reply. "Do I look like I need a nap? I need another nap like I need another pain in my neck! I want to go *do* something!" Frances is shouting, and I wheel her quickly into her room, away from the ears of the retiring lunch crowd. She trembles in her sudden anger. "I'm sick and tired of being stuck here and told what to do!" Frances grabs hold of the sides of her wheelchair, which I've just locked in place, and begins to lift herself up out of the chair.

"Whoa! Hang on Frances," I soothe. "You're not gonna be able to go anywhere if you fall." She ignores me and reaches for her walker.

"Then let me fall! I'm gonna go where I damn well please, or die trying." She struggles to her feet and takes a wobbly step forward. I stand behind her, tensed and ready for her legs to give out from under her.

"Frances, please, be reasonable. Sit down before you hurt yourself." I gently coax the walker out of her insistent grip and ease her into her armchair. Frances sits stiffly. She looks at me, defeated, and begins a silent stream of tears.

"Frances, I know you want to go out, and I would give anything to see you up and enjoying yourself. But I can't watch you hurt yourself and end up in more pain."

"I just want to be able to go see my nephew," she mourns. "I miss them all so much. Before, I could do whatever I wanted. And now, look at me...I can't even get out of my chair

Elizabeth Lombardo
Walpole, ME

without your help." Frances stares out the window, clearly willing herself to be somewhere else. Tears continue to roll down the side of her face. "I used to have such fun."

"What'd you used to do, when you were younger?" I ask, hoping to distract her.

"What?" Frances slowly returns from her reverie. "What'd I used to do? Oh, this and that—a hell of a lot more than I do now." She reaches for the worn photo album in the pocket of her recliner. "Here, I'll show you."

***

Frances and I spend the rest of the afternoon looking at pictures. To listen to her reminisce is to watch her worries and pain float away. She smiles. She laughs. She tells me the most wild stories of her escapades as a young girl, defying authority and causing trouble. I can't believe some of them. And when she speaks of her family, the pride in her voice— it's clear she loves them more than anything. The joy held in her memories, the pleasure of being able to share them. Frances is no longer the sick and hopeless woman I started my shift with. She's sprung to life like the first flowers of spring. She might be stuck in a failing body, in a dull, lifeless place, going through the motions of her everyday routine, but there's more to her than that. The joys she's found as a child, a young woman, a matriarch—these live on with her even while her health and family fade away. She still lives for the joy she once had, the joy she can still find no matter what her circumstances.

That evening, I help Frances get ready for bed as usual. However, when it's time to move her from the bathroom into bed, I don't wheel her over. I hand Frances her walker and take a step back.

"Here," I say.

"Huh?" She gives me a quizzical look.

"You're a tough, independent old bird. Walk yourself to

Elizabeth Lombardo
Walpole, ME

bed. Just don't run. It's not like that time you got caught smoking in your college dorm. You don't have to hide from me."

"Ha!" she smiles. "You liked that story, huh? I can be a rebel when I want to be!"

"I'd no idea," I reply. I stand behind her as she proudly waddles to the bed, a wry grin on my face.

Pain

My night shifts with Frances begin at six, but I'm late today because I stopped by the cemetery. I'm thinking of how much I miss my college roommate, and how beautiful her two little girls are becoming, when I finally arrive at Frances's room at twelve minutes past six.

I walk through the door, knocking as I enter. The room is dark and quiet—odd for this time of evening. From the light of the open door, I can make out her bed, neatly made, and her couch and chair waiting expectantly with their piles of cushions. But where is Frances? At dinner? But the dinner hour should be well over by now. Curious, I walk further into the small room. "Where is that woman?" I wonder aloud as I cross past her bed.

"Oh my, God! Frances!" My patient's fragile body is sprawled out on the floor at the side of her bed. My outburst does not wake her. I kneel down beside her and gently reach for her hand, dreading the possibility of finding it stiff and cold.

"Thank God!" I stammer, my worries put to rest by the weak, but warm pulse that meets my fingers. "Are you trying to scare the crap out of me?"

Frances's lids flutter open for a fraction of a second, acknowledging my presence. Not impressed, I continue, "What'd you think you're doing down here?"

"Go away." It's barely a breath.

"What's that?" I say, settling down beside her to hear better.

Elizabeth Lombardo
Walpole, ME

"Leave me alone," comes the hoarse, but firm reply.

"But Frances, I'm here to help you," I explain gently. "What are you doing down here? Did you fall?" It seems the likeliest explanation, whether she's going to admit it or not.

Frances shakes her head from side to side without opening her eyes, an infinitesimal movement that seems to carry the weight of eighty years. "I want to die," she whispers. "Leave me alone. I just want to be left in peace, so I can die."

"No, Frances. It's not time for you to die yet. You're just having a bad day. Come on and let me help you up. Then we'll get you something to make you feel better."

I rub her arm, willing her to find the motivation to move. As I caress the delicate tissue paper of her skin, I notice the perfect placement of the pillows behind her head and the incessant *chug-puff* of oxygen that's supplying the room instead of her nostrils from where it lies on her bedspread. It seems defiantly set aside. *Maybe she's "fallen" on purpose*, I think. I open my mouth to say "Come on," but she cuts me off before the words can fully escape my mouth.

"No! Get out!" Frances commands with more vehemence and force than I'd have thought possible two seconds before. "Get the hell out of here! I don't want you, so just get the hell out of here and let me die!" She is ready to be done, and she is going to stick to her guns until either the devil or the angels come to carry her away. She shakes as she speaks; then—slowly—the wave of her anger folds back in on itself, the shaking subsides, and she is still.

"Frances," I whisper in her ear. "Frances, I'm not going to let you die. Not tonight. God will tell you when it's time. And He can find you in your bed just as well as He can find you on the floor." I adjust myself at her side so I can look into her eyes, still shut against my presence. "I'm going to help you get into bed and then get you some medicine to help your pain and make it easier for you to breathe, okay? But I need you to listen to me. You're going to do what I say and take care of yourself because it's the right thing to do. Not

Elizabeth Lombardo
Walpole, ME

because I'm being mean or bossy."

I gaze down at her, my expression concerned, but every bit as determined as hers. I lean in to kiss her forehead, bringing on a quiet flow of tears that silently make their way down the side of her face. Whether from pain, or frustration, or resignation, I'll never know. They're gone by the time I've rung for a second nurse to help hoist her tired frame back into bed. After a good dose of morphine and a nebulizer to aid her breathing, she is still too distressed to speak to me before she falls asleep. So I sit by her bedside, useless, as she slowly allows the medicine to overwhelm her senses and carry her to sleep.

***

Now that it's quiet, I'm left to ponder the sanity of this world. Hours ago, I was at the grave of my beloved friend, a woman taken away suddenly from her husband and children, all because someone hadn't stopped in time at a crosswalk. I can still see Rebekah's face now—so vibrant in life, so anguished at the hospital, so pale at her wake. How did this woman, who had so much life left to live, so much more left to give those who loved her—how did she get taken away when this painfully ill shadow beside me has been praying to take her place? It's so backward.

To those who say we don't die until we've fulfilled some greater purpose, what purpose has Frances not fulfilled? What heavenly or earthly plan has not yet come to fruition while she lies here, confused and in pain, day after day, week after week? And how much more could my friend have fulfilled if she had lived? What blessings and lessons could she have offered to her children and her children's children, had she been granted the opportunity?

Who knows? All I know is that life is for living. It seems a waste to spend it dying.

Elizabeth Lombardo
Walpole, ME

Epilogue

There isn't much time to get close to my patients. My life is a constant flow of new patients and new charts, coming to me through the unceasing revolving door that is time. That's how it is in geriatrics. I assumed that's how it'd be with Frances.

Frances died on a Saturday. Well, she really didn't give up until the following Monday, but I don't consider a morphine drip any sort of life. Once the drugs kicked in and caught up with her, it was nothing but morphine induced sleep until the very end.

Waiting was agony. It was like she was drowning slowly, but was so used to swimming that she couldn't allow herself to take the first gulp of water and drink in death. And there I sat, I who had been her lifeboat for the past few months; I sat there and cried as she floundered out of my reach.

Something had happened over the last few months. Something about our time together had gotten to me. She wasn't just another chart, one more hand to hold and heart to comfort before exiting through the revolving door. Frances had shared the last of her life with me, shown vibrancy I'd never seen before in my fading patients. The end of her chart would not mean the end of our connection.

It's over now for her, for Frances. But I know it's not over for me. I still have time before it's my turn to exit this world through the revolving door and enter into eternity. God knows I'm certainly not ready yet. When I am, though, I hope I'll exit like my friend Frances, who basked in the joy of life, in spite of all its pain, hopeful right up to the end.

Thomas Peter Bennett
Silver Spring, MD

Catbird

Your soft meowing
        floats on April breezes.

Welcome back from
        your Florida trip,
now that spring
        has begun.

Enjoy hiding in
        your favorite greening
thickets and serenading
        with trills and purrs.

***

Mary Ann Bedwell
Grants, NM

A Study in Negative Space

Shadows slide silently along the ground,
dead trees cast silhouettes on a wall.

Something scurries, scattering the leaves,
sentinel evergreens cast their pall.

The echo of footsteps from the empty street
goads me into a more frantic pace.

Being afraid of what's not there—
a study in negative space!

GOOSE RIVER ANTHOLOGY, 2021

We seek selections of fine poetry, essays, and short stories (3,000 words or less) for the 19th annual *Goose River Anthology, 2021.* The book will be beautifully produced with full color cover and full color hard covers.

You may submit even if you have been published before in a previous edition of the *Goose River Anthology.* We retain one-time publishing rights. All rights revert back to the author after publication. You may submit as many pieces as you like.

EARN CASH ROYALTIES. Author will receive a 10% royalty on all sales that he or she generates.

There is no purchase required and nothing is required of the author for publication. Deadline for submissions is April 30, 2021. Publication will be in the fall of 2021 (they make great Christmas gifts). Guidelines are as follows:

- Submit clean, typed copy by snail mail—**mandatory**
- Email a Word, rtf, or PDF file to us (if possible)
- Reading fee: $1.00 per page
- Do not put two poems on the same page
- Essays and short stories **must be** double-spaced
- **SASE (#10 or larger) for notification** (one forever stamp) plus additional postage for possible return of submission if desired.
- Author's name & address at top of each page of paper copy and first page of emailed copies.

Submit to:
Goose River Anthology, 2021
3400 Friendship Road
Waldoboro, ME 04572-6337
Email: gooseriverpress@gmail.com
www.gooseriverpress.com